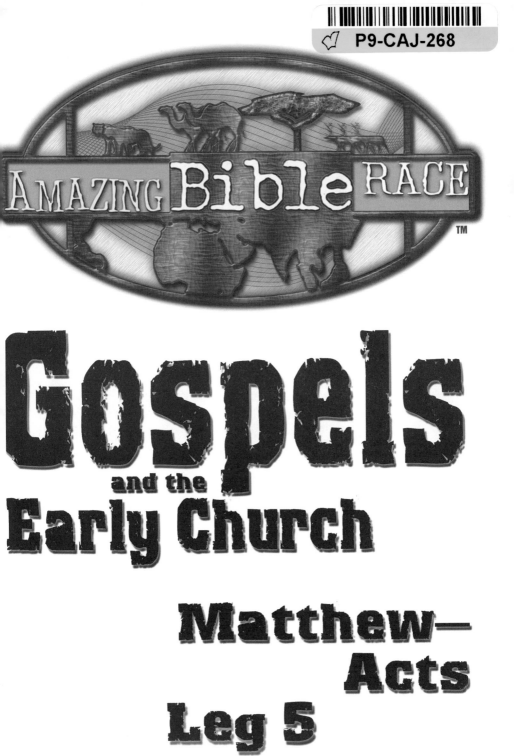

AMAZING Bible RACE ™

Gospels
and the
Early Church

Matthew—
Acts
Leg 5

08 09 10 11 12 13 14 15 16 17—10 9 8 7 6 5 4 3 2 1

Cover Design: Keely Moore

Contents

Race Map...4

On to a New Testament.............................6

Week 1...8

Week 2...18

Week 3...28

Week 4...38

Week 5...48

Week 6...58

Week 7...68

Week 8...78

Week 9...88

Week 10...98

Week 11...108

Week 12...118

Amazing Bible Race Team Covenant........128

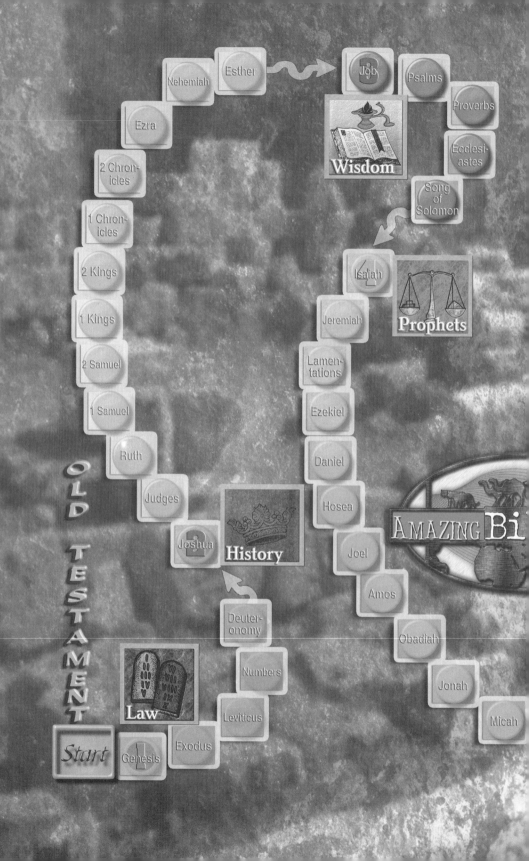

© 2007 by Abingdon Youth

On to a New Testament

Now that you've completed all 39 books of the Old Testament, it's time for something new. Welcome to the New Testament, where you will learn the story of Jesus and the early church. When the New Testament begins, more than 500 years have passed since the people of Judah returned from exile and rebuilt the Temple. Although much has changed (the Romans are in control now), the New Testament, like the Old, tells a story of love, grace, and redemption.

As you continue the Race, keep a few things in mind:

1. **Be a team player**—Teamwork is essential to the Amazing Bible Race. Don't be afraid to ask for help from a teammate and be willing to offer your help to the rest of your team.

2. **Give it your all**—If you ever become discouraged or overwhelmed, just think about how far you've come and how much you've learned. Keep digging and keep learning. Don't give up!

3. **Focus on the journey, not on the prize**—While the Amazing Bible Race has points, prizes, and a finish line, reading and studying Scripture is a life-long task. The true objective of this Race is not to beat other teams or to win a grand prize—in this Leg you will hear Jesus say that the "first will be last, and the last will be first" (Matthew 19:30)—but to meet God in Scripture daily and to learn about God's will for the world. Don't get so wrapped up in the competition that you lose sight of what's important.

4. **Use a Bible translation that you understand**—If you still haven't found a Bible translation that you're comfortable with, try something else. If you'd prefer a Bible written in contemporary language, try the *Contemporary English Version* or *Today's New International Version*. If you're looking for something more scholarly, go with the *New Revised Standard Version* or the *New International Version*. Websites such as *bible.crosswalk.com, www.biblegateway.com,* and *bible.oremus.org* allow you to search within and read from several translations. You might also choose to listen to Scripture. (For free MP3 files, search key words "free Bible MP3" to locate various free MP3 downloads. Then choose the version that you like best.)

Amazing Bible RACE ™

The Rules

Rule 1
Follow steps 1–4 for each daily reading.

Rule 2
As a team, answer the Weekly Challenges and submit them to the website.

Rule 3
Accomplish any Fast Forwards that appear in your Runner's Reader. A Fast Forward appears periodically and is a life-application exercise for your team. You'll be asked to find a way to apply the Bible reading to your life. For example, if you're reading about feeding the hungry, you might decide to serve food at a local rescue mission. To receive credit for the outing, you must have someone make a video of it or take a photo of your group in action; then upload it to *amazingbiblerace.com.*

Rule 4
Help your teammates overcome any Hurdles. When you face a particularly difficult section of Scripture or feel that you're getting stuck, you might see a Hurdle. Hurdles allow you to skim that particular Scripture passage and accomplish or perform a task based on the Bible lesson or solve a quiz on *amazingbiblerace.com* to "quiz-out" of that section.

Rule 5
Earn as many points as possible for your team. You gain points by finishing your daily readings, solving Weekly Challenges, participating in the Fast Forwards, solving the extra quizzes, or looking on the map and taking a quiz. The more effort you put in to the Race, the more you'll get out of it—and the more points you'll receive!

Rule 6
The adult mentor is the team coach who keeps team members encouraged and motivated. The coach should check in at least once a week to make sure that everyone is reading and that you have a time scheduled to work together (by IM, e-mail, text message, or phone conversation) to solve the Weekly Challenge.

Rule 7
Support your team and work together.

Rule 8
Have fun!

The Rest of the Story
Matthew 1–2

1 Scouting the Terrain

For many readers, the Bible's New Testament is like a breath of fresh air. We've read through the sometimes difficult and sometimes repetitive Old Testament. While we believe that all of God's Word is beneficial, many Christians have a special affinity for the New Testament.

The Gospels, the first four New Testament books, present the fulfillment of God's grand plan of redemption in the person and work of Jesus Christ. We read of the mission and growth of the early church in Acts. We are exhorted and encouraged by the words of men and women devoted to Christ. One of the Bible's most popular and prolific writers, Paul, has a dramatic conversion from darkness to light and is responsible for several New Testament writings that give guidance and encouragement to Christians then and now. In Revelation, the New Testament's final book, we get a glimpse of the glory that awaits those who believe.

Welcome to the rest of the story!

Trailblazers

• **Jesus**
• **Mary**
• **Joseph**
• **angel of the Lord**
• **wise men**
• **King Herod**

• What sorts of things did you learn about God by reading the Old Testament?

• What about the New Testament do you most look forward to?

2 NOW READ MATTHEW 1–2.

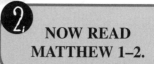

③ Switchback

Mary, Jesus' mother, was favored among women—not because of her virginity but because of her love for God. Matthew tells us that Mary's conceiving, although she remained a virgin, was a fulfillment of Isaiah 7:14. This miracle birth shows the world that God can do the impossible.

Modern humanity's continual pursuit of knowledge and scientific proof leaves little room for the impossible or the miraculous. Consider Jesus' relationship to miracles. His own birth is a result of a miracle. He performs a variety of miracles throughout the Gospels. He rises miraculously from the dead.

• If the Christmas story had taken place in the twenty-first century, what do you think Mary's response would have been? Joseph's? society's? Joseph and Mary's parents?

• Why, do you think, is Jesus' birth in a stable significant?

Road Signs

• **genealogy:** This word literally means "origin or beginning," as in the word *genesis*. In biblical terminology, the word could also mean "account," as in the "account of the beginning of Jesus Christ."

④ Prayer

Lord, grant us the strength and the patience to wait on the fulfillment of your divine promises made to us revealed in the life of Jesus Christ. Amen.

Study the events surrounding Jesus' birth in Matthew 1–2. Connect the New Testament events with Old Testament prophecies about the coming Messiah. Take a quiz at *amazingbiblerace.com* to see how much you've learned.

Opening Act
Matthew 3–4

1 Scouting the Terrain

Before the main attraction performs, the audience must sit through the opening act. The job of concert openers is to warm up the audience for the star of the show. Most entertainers booked as opening acts don't mind the job, because they feel honored being on the same stage as the star of the show.

This is John the Baptist's attitude as he prepares the way for Jesus. He points to the headlining act by baptizing people and urging them to repent of their sins. Ultimately, John has the honor of baptizing Jesus himself.

• Why was John the Baptist's work so important for the ministry of Jesus?

Trailblazers

• John the Baptist
• Jesus
• Satan
• Simon Peter
• Andrew
• James son of Zebedee
• John

• How do you point people toward Jesus?

2 NOW READ MATTHEW 3–4.

3 Switchback

John the Baptist was a little weird. OK, a lot weird. Making his home in the wilderness, dining on grasshoppers, and wearing sack cloth made this Messianic messenger stand out in a crowd.

His differences, though, did not keep people from hearing and receiving his message.

Too often, we are quick to judge others based on the ways they dress or speak without really hearing what they have to say. Sadly, such prejudice can push these people to the outermost fringes of society. John the Baptist, whom God chose as the person who would "Prepare the way of the Lord," is proof that even the strangest people can speak profound and important truths.

- Describe how John the Baptist might look and dress today. How would people react to his message?

- When have you made judgments about a person based on his or her appearance? What opportunities for relationships have you missed because of these hasty judgments?

Road Signs

- **repent:** This is the first command of both John and Jesus. Repentance is not just sorrow for committing a sin but a decision to change, to turn from sin toward obedience.

Pace Pusher

Matthew 4:1-11 is the story of Jesus' temptation in the wilderness. In verse 6, Satan quotes Scripture but uses Psalm 91:11-12 in a way contrary the psalmist's intent. How does knowing this about Satan's tactics affect the way you study Scripture?

4 Prayer

Dear God, help us follow the examples you have set before us. Let us remember that when we fall short of your grace, you are present and ready to forgive us. Amen.

Blessed Are Those ...
Matthew 5–7

1 Scouting the Terrain

Parallels between Jesus and Moses become apparent as Jesus preaches the Sermon on the Mount. Moses received the Law on Mt. Sinai and gave it to the Israelites from the mountain; Jesus preaches a sermon from the mountain in which he reiterates these Ten Commandments but goes deeper.

The sermon opens with the Beatitudes. On first reading, one may think that Jesus is simply feeling sorry for those who are disadvantaged or downtrodden. While Jesus is certainly full of compassion for the weak, his words have a deeper spiritual meaning. Jesus commends those who are sorrowful over their sin, are submissive to God, and seek God's righteousness. Persons who behave in this manner grow closer to God and will receive the blessings mentioned.

This sermon also includes the Golden Rule (7:12): "Do unto others as you would have them do unto you."

Trailblazers

- **Jesus**
- **Jesus' disciples**
- **the crowds**

• Make a list of the Beatitudes. Why, do you think, does Jesus open the Sermon on the Mount with these blessings?

2 NOW READ MATTHEW 5–7.

3 Switchback

Readers sometimes assume that, by telling his followers to "turn the other cheek" (5:39), Jesus is telling his followers to be weak and passive. In fact, the opposite is true. Jesus is telling us not to sink to the level of our attacker by fighting back but also not running away from adversity. Instead, we should be strong and courageous when someone strikes us, letting that person know that we will not be intimidated and having the strength and courage not to fight back. This teaching and those that follow it have become the cornerstone of the nonviolent resistance practiced by leaders such as Martin Luther King, Jr.

Jesus' countercultural teachings continue as he instructs us to "Love [our] enemies and pray for those who persecute [us]" (5:44). Anyone can love family and friends. Loving an enemy takes true courage and character.

All of Jesus' teachings in the Sermon on the Mount point to a way of life that is often at odds with the culture in which we live. It is a lifestyle of humility and generosity, of self-control and high moral standards, and of strength in the face of adversity.

• When have you had the most difficulty "turning the other cheek"? Why are people often tempted to fight back?

• How might the world change if everyone were to faithfully follow the teachings in the Sermon on the Mount?

4 Prayer

Radical Teacher, give us the strength and courage to follow your teachings, especially when doing so is countercultural. Amen.

That's a Miracle!
Matthew 8–9

1 Scouting the Terrain

After preaching a sermon for the ages, Jesus comes down from the mountain and begins his ministry of healing. He heals a leper then goes into Capernaum (the fishing village where he has made his home—see 4:13), where he heals a Roman soldier's servant. He goes on to heal Peter's mother-in-law, two demon-possessed men, a hemorrhaging woman, two blind men, and a man who cannot speak. He even raises a recently deceased girl to life.

Through these healings and other amazing feats such as stopping a storm, Jesus shows that miracles are not just magical stunts. God's miracles require faith. Jesus' miraculous acts are extraordinary signs that point to God's miraculous ability to bring life from death.

• Why, do you think, did Jesus perform miracles as part of his earthly ministry?

WEEK
1
◆
DAY
4

• Is your Christian belief strengthened, weakened, or unaffected by studying Jesus' miracles? Why?

Trailblazers

• Jesus
• crowds
• persons who needed to be healed of leprosy, demon possession, paralysis, hemorrhaging, blindness, muteness, and even death
• a centurion
• Peter's mother-in-law
• the disciples

2 NOW READ MATTHEW 8–9.

3 Switchback

Where are God's miracles today? We have all witnessed sickness, death, and widespread destruction in our lives and the lives of others. So why hasn't God intervened? Because we know that God is capable of performing incredible miracles, we are confused when a loved one is sick or dies or when disaster causes harm to people's lives and kills thousands of people.

Many Christians would maintain that God still performs miracles, even if those miracles aren't as obvious as those we read about in the Gospels. Some claim to have witnessed miraculous healings similar to those that Jesus performs in today's reading. Others believe that miracles today come in the form of incredible technological advancements. Still others see miracles every day in nature, in the arts, and in extraordinary acts of human kindness.

• What miracles have you witnessed? What made them miraculous?

Road Signs

• **leprosy:** A variety of skin diseases could have been called, "leprosy." The most dominant form was a disfiguring bacterial infection that attacks the skin and nerves.

• **centurion:** This was the rank of an officer in the Roman army who was in charge of 100 soldiers.

• Why, do you think, does God not intervene more often to miraculously save people who have been hurt by disease or natural disasters?

4 Prayer

Dear God, increase our faith so that while we live out your will, we can fully embrace your power and authority that makes lame people walk, blind people see, and deaf people hear. Amen.

Called to Follow
Matthew 10–11

1 Scouting the Terrain

Jesus sends the twelve apostles out with a mission: to proclaim the "good news" of the "kingdom of heaven" (10:7) to the "lost sheep of the house of Israel" (10:6). In other words, for the time being, Jesus wants the disciples to preach to Jews rather than Gentiles. Jesus himself gives the disciples authority to heal and cast out demons. He specifically tells the disciples to take no material possessions with them. Instead, they are to depend entirely on God's provision through those to whom they minister.

Trailblazers

- Jesus
- the twelve apostles
- John the Baptist

Jesus also prepares his disciples for rejection by warning them that some of the people to whom they minister will reject and mistreat them. Jesus says—Don't fear. Don't take it personally. It's not about you; it's about me.

- Why would Jesus require the twelve to leave material possessions at home and, instead, depend on God's provision?

- How does Jesus challenge and empower us today to proclaim the good news of his kingdom?

2 NOW READ MATTHEW 10–11.

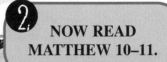

3 Switchback

Have you been teased or ridiculed for "doing the right thing"? Have you been made fun of for your belief in Christ? Have you been looked down upon for choosing to attend church or a church event when some other school or sporting event is happening at the same time?

Jesus warned that following him would not be easy. He told the disciples that they would be going out as "sheep into the midst of wolves" (10:16). What do wolves do to sheep? Eat them alive.

Growing up as a Christian in today's culture is not easy. Christians often find themselves at odds with cultural trends that aren't grounded in God's word. Fortunately, Jesus, through the Holy Spirit, continues to assure us, saying, "Do not be afraid" (10:31).

• When has ridicule or the fear of ridicule made it difficult for you to remain true to your faith?

• What happens to Christ's message when people who claim to be Christians give into pressure and act in ways that don't honor God?

4 Prayer

O Lord, I know that I am a vulnerable sheep among hungry wolves. Equip me to spread your kingdom message with boldness. Amen.

Water Break

The word *gospel* means "good news." The good news now is that the second half of Matthew's Gospel is even more exciting than the first!

It's the Law! Or Is It?
Matthew 12–13

1 Scouting the Terrain

The Pharisees were obsessed with keeping God's law. They had a very strict and specific interpretation of how the Law should be observed. And the Pharisees' view of the Law certainly does not allow picking and eating grain on the sabbath, which is exactly what Jesus' disciples are doing. Plucking, after all, is work, and the Law requires rest on the sabbath.

Jesus has a different understanding of the Law. He explains that the Law must always be interpreted in light of the Lawgiver. The Lawgiver's intention is to foster a relationship between God and humans. Obsessing over the details of certain rules just for the sake of appearing righteous does not accomplish God's purpose.

Trailblazers

• **Jesus**
• **Disciples**
• **Pharisees**
• **Jesus' mother and brothers**
• **Crowds**

• Is Jesus changing God's rule about the sabbath? Why, or why not?

• How does following God's law bring us closer to God?

• What is dangerous about obsessing over the details of certain rules?

2 NOW READ MATTHEW 12–13.

3 Switchback

We humans love rules. We like to know when we've performed to the coach's expectations. We like to know when we've finished our chores so that we can go out with friends. We'd love to be able to know that we've pleased God in every thought, word, and deed every single second of each day.

Living the Christian life with a "do this" but "don't do this" checklist appeals to our human nature. But Jesus doesn't want us to keep a checklist. Instead, he wants us to focus on our heart and our relationship with God. If we do that, we will be like good trees that bear good fruit (12:33-35), and we will speak and act in ways that are pleasing to God.

• In what ways can you focus on your relationship with God so that you will bear "good fruit"?

4 Prayer

Lord, give me wisdom to embrace your grace and mercy. Amen.

fast forward

Debates rage in the church about what is a faithful interpretation of Scripture. In today's Scripture, Jesus and the Pharisees disagree on the proper interpretation of the commandment to keep the sabbath holy. Today, Christians debate the meaning of the Bible's teaching on issues such as war, drinking alcohol, homosexuality, gambling, the death penalty, and worship style.

Invite your pastor to speak to your group about how your congregation and denomination have debated some of these issues and what conclusions have been reached.

Make a video based on what you've learned and upload it at *amazingbiblerace.com*. It could be a newscast, video diary, or music video, but it must deal with at least two cultural or church-related topics.

Road Sign

• **Pharisee** (FAIR-uh-see)**:** This was the leadership group among the Jewish people who were concerned with legalism and separatism and believed strongly in the resurrection of the dead.

A Miracle Dinner
Matthew 14

① Scouting the Terrain

Chapter 14 opens with the horrific beheading of John the Baptist. Upon hearing of John's death, Jesus needs some alone time. He seeks a solitary place, away from the hustle and bustle that has come to characterize his ministry.

But it doesn't take long for the crowds to catch up to him. Even though Jesus is grieving, he heals those in the crowd who are seeking his help. Then Jesus goes one step farther. Even though his disciples suggest that he send away the crowds in the evening (after all, it is getting close to dinnertime), Jesus decides to feed their bodies, as well as their souls.

From five loaves of bread and two fish, Jesus feeds a crowd of five thousand men and thousands more women and children. The leftovers even fill twelve baskets!

• How do you react when people interrupt you while you are trying to have some time to yourself?

Trailblazers

- John the Baptist
- Herod
- Herodias' daughter
- Jesus
- the disciples
- the crowd
- Peter

• What is impressive about how Jesus acts in this Scripture?

② NOW READ MATTHEW 14.

3 Switchback

When have you been really hungry? Think about what it feels like to go a few hours or a few days without a meal.

The crowds in today's passage are hungry on two levels. They have spiritual needs and physical needs. They need healing for their souls and their bodies. Jesus, although certainly distraught by John the Baptist's death, has pity on the people. In a "deserted place" (14:13), he meets their needs with his touch of healing and his abundance of food.

Sometimes God calls us to a place of wilderness, with no distractions but our restless spirits and our growling tummies. In these times, we are dependent on Jesus alone. In these places, we are able to receive the healing from one whose compassion is never ending.

• Why are the wilderness times of life so important to our growth as Christians?

Road Signs

- **Herodias:** She was Herod's niece and the wife of his half-brother Philip, so Herod's relationship with her was incestuous. In those days, rulers often used marriages to build alliances and expand control.
- **"deserted place"** (14:15): This scene of Jesus providing food for the 5,000 in this remote location recalls the scene of God providing manna in the desert (Exodus 16) and Elisha's miracle (2 Kings 4:42-44).
- **"early in the morning"** (14:25): Some translations say, "fourth watch," 3:00 a.m. to 6:00 a.m.

4 Prayer

O merciful and wise God, when I am in the wilderness again, remind me to reach to you for nourishment. Amen.

Power from the "Crumbs"
Matthew 15–16

1 Scouting the Terrain

Prior to the Resurrection, the "dividing wall" (see Ephesians 2:14) between Gentiles and Jews still stood. Jesus had come specifically for the lost of house of Israel, yet the Canaanite woman (a Gentile) comes to him asking for her daughter's healing.

Cultural, ethnic, political, economic, and religious barriers all are at work in this scene. But we soon see how God has the power to transcend them all. Jesus responds to the Canaanite woman and commends her faith once she makes known that she, as a non-Jew, does not feel entitled to the benefits of the covenant mercies. Instead, she has faith that she could benefit from the overflow of the blessings promised to Israel. She recognized the powerful abundance of healing that was included in even the tiniest morsel of the spillover of God's gracious acts.

• What do you find most interesting about the Canaanite woman's conversation with Jesus? What does this story tell us about our relationship with Christ?

Trailblazers

- Pharisees
- teachers of the Law
- Jesus
- the crowds
- the Canaanite woman
- Sadducees
- the disciples
- Peter

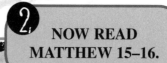

2 NOW READ MATTHEW 15–16.

3 Switchback

You deserve it. You've worked hard. You are entitled to a place on the basketball team, an academic free-ride scholarship to the college of your choice, a brand-new sports car on your sixteenth birthday.

In the western world today, many people grow up feeling entitled to health, wealth, happiness, and prosperity. When real life slaps us in the face, though, we get a taste of how much of the rest of the world lives.

The Canaanite woman in today's passage has a truly humble heart. She knows that she is outside the bounds of God's covenant promises to the people of Israel. She is not entitled to anything. Her faith, however, is so great and her heart is so hungry that she longs for just a nibble at the overflow of Jesus' blessings. She has faith that even the tiniest leftover will nourish and sustain her and meet all of her needs.

Without Christ, we all are outside the bounds of God's promises and abundant blessings. Without Christ, we are entitled to nothing. Only by his grace do we feast at the table.

• How hungry are you for "crumbs" of Jesus' blessing?

Road Signs

• **Sadducee** (SAD-joo-see): This was the party of the traditional ruling class of priests in Judaism. The Sadducees rejected any beliefs or actions that weren't in the Law and did not believe in the resurrection of the dead.
• **Gentile** (GEN-tyl): This was a person of a non-Jewish nation or of non-Jewish faith.
• **Canaanite** (KAY-nuh-nite): This was a name for ancient Israel's neighboring pagan enemies. In Jesus' time, this term was sometimes used to mean "Gentile."

4 Prayer

Lord, give us hungry, believing, and faithful hearts. Amen.

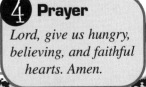

23

Like a Child
Matthew 17–18

1 Scouting the Terrain

Trailblazers

- Jesus
- Peter
- James
- John
- Moses
- Elijah
- a boy with a demon
- the disciples

"Who is the greatest?" The disciples wanted to know Jesus' answer and were surely shocked when he called a child, as an example, to come to him.

Jesus commands the disciples to become as children. He does not mean the innocence or purity of children. Instead, Jesus highlights their dependence, their powerlessness, and their vulnerability.

The disciples, who were accustomed to living in a hierarchical society, must have been surprised. Once again, Jesus refutes any assumptions they (or other hearers or future readers) would have about possessing societal standing, wealth, power, or intelligence.

Nothing that society values impresses God. Nothing humans can offer impresses God. Those who cling to God and to God alone are "greatest" in the kingdom.

•Why, do you think, did the disciples approach Jesus with the question?

2 NOW READ MATTHEW 17–18.

③ Switchback

Our culture gives awards for everything. Schools honor valedictorians; sports leagues name their most valuable players; the film and music industries hold flashy awards shows to recognize their best and brightest. As a culture, we enjoy celebrating a job well done.

God's kingdom, however, has different criteria for recognition. God isn't impressed by human status symbols. In today's passage, Jesus tells the disciples that they must become as little children to enter the kingdom of heaven. In other words, we must trust in Christ the way a child follows a parent.

• What awards or accolades are most important to you? Why are they so important?

• How might trying to win recognition from others get in the way of your relationship with God?

The Book of Matthew portrays children in vulnerable states. Look for descriptions of children in the following chapters: 2, 8, 9, 14, 15, and 17. Consider how these descriptions of children give more depth to Jesus' teaching in today's passage. Take a quiz at *amazingbiblerace.com* to see how much you have learned.

④ Prayer

God our Father, give us the faith of children. Amen.

Through the Eye of a Needle
Matthew 19–20

1 Scouting the Terrain

One can almost imagine the rich young man's urgency in approaching Jesus with his burning question about having eternal life. "Now, I'll know," he thought, perhaps. "Now, I'll get it straight from the source exactly what I need to do to be right with God and go to heaven."

But Jesus upsets his expectations. Jesus tells him to keep all of the commandments. The rich young man says that he does, but he wants to know what more is required. So Jesus gets to the heart of the issue: the man's love of his possessions. Certainly, the man wasn't expecting Jesus to tell him to sell his possessions and give the money to the poor. The man walks away, grieving. He just can't bear to lose his stuff.

• What would it take for the man to sell his possessions and give the money to the poor?

Trailblazers

- Jesus
- the crowds
- Pharisees
- little children
- a rich young man
- the disciples
- Peter
- the mother of Zebedee's sons
- Zebedee's sons
- two blind men

WEEK
2
❖
DAY
5

• Do you think that the man did as Jesus commanded? Why, or why not?

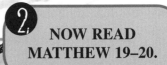

2 NOW READ MATTHEW 19–20.

③ Switchback

Have you seen any of those "clutter-busting" television shows? The host, usually skilled at organizing, helps a family clean up their houses and get rid of an abundance of stuff. Many talk shows also deal with the problem of clutter, often inviting psychologists to talk about the true affliction of hoarding.

The rich young man in today's passage has accumulated many things. He has been able to buy anything he wants, and he loves his stuff. He also wants eternal life and decides that Jesus can tell him exactly how to get it. Since he is accustomed to getting anything he wants, he is shocked when Jesus exposes the one thing that he's not willing (or able) to do: give up his stuff. He's grieved when he leaves Jesus. His heart is powerfully attached to his possessions, since he is more willing to leave Jesus than lose his stuff.

• Which possessions would you have the hardest time giving up? How might your love of these possessions be affecting your relationship with God?

Fast Forward

Have a Christian psychologist speak to your team about hoarding and the emotional and spiritual connections to loving stuff more than loving God. As a team, watch a TV show about clutter-busting (*Clean House, Clean Sweep,* and so forth). Apply what you've learned to a "stuff situation" in your life or someone else's. Create a video in which you do a "clean sweep" of your own, then upload the video to *amazingbiblerace.com*.

④ Prayer

Dear God, I don't want to love anything more than I love you. Refocus my heart's priorities. Amen.

Water Break

Keep moving and get ready for some of the most exciting chapters in the Bible.

Trick Questions
Matthew 21–23

1 Scouting the Terrain

Jesus enters Jerusalem to shouts of joy and praise. Meanwhile, the Pharisees and scribes plot against him. They don't like the way the crowd supports Jesus. They find it threatening. With one voice, the crowd welcomes Jesus, waving palms and praising him as the one who comes in the name of the Lord. The power of the crowd is not in the volume of their voices but in their ability to be in one truthful accord shouting in unison: "Hosanna! Hosanna!"

As Jesus teaches in Jerusalem, the Pharisees and the Sadducees continually try to trip him up by asking trick questions. Jesus, however, skillfully skirts their manipulation, speaks the truth, and exposes their intent.

Trailblazers

• Jesus
• the disciples
• the crowd
• chief priests
  and teachers
  of Law

• Why, do you think, does Jesus arrive on a donkey rather than in a more glorified manner?

• Why, do you think, did the Pharisees see Jesus as a threat?

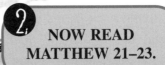

**NOW READ
MATTHEW 21–23.**

③ Switchback

Jesus is Truth incarnate. In a few weeks, you'll read in John 8:31, where Jesus proclaims that, " 'If you continue in my word, you are truly my disciples; and you will know the truth, and the truth will make you free.' "

Abiding in, proclaiming, and clinging to the truth is always liberating. Jesus is always able to brilliantly maneuver around the Pharisees' attempts at deception because he proclaims and never wavers from the truth. He's not concerned with pretenses or impressions. He's concerned with doing God's will.

Sometimes truth is hard to identify in our culture. Remember, though, that Jesus says that his teachings are truth. Believe them, and they will set you free.

• How does truth set us free?

• How do lies trap and imprison us?

Road Signs

• **"outer darkness, where there will be weeping and gnashing of teeth"** (8:12; 22:13; 25:30): This refers to the punishment at the final judgment.
• **"all the law and the prophets"** (22:40): This refers to the entire Old Testament.
• **gnat** and **camel:** These are the smallest and largest of the unclean animals.

④ Prayer

O Lord, how excellent you are! Let our mouths be filled with Hosannas and our hearts be filled with humility so that we can worship you in spirit and in truth. Amen.

Riddle Me This
Matthew 24–25

1 Scouting the Terrain

The Riddler from the Batman stories mixes it up for our caped crusader. He leaves strange clues for Batman about where he will strike next. Cleverly rhymed in the form of riddles, his clues are no match for Batman. In no time, he figures them out and is off to foil The Riddler's plans for destruction.

To the disciples, Jesus may as well be speaking in riddles. Jesus' parables are full of symbolism and embedded messages. Upon first hearing them, the disciples do not fully appreciate the message of the parables. The disciples don't understand that Jesus is talking about his death, his resurrection, and God's final victory.

Trailblazers

• Jesus
• the disciples

He encourages his disciples to be strong even after his death. Jesus warns that there will be much suffering to come, but those who believe ultimately will be blessed. He also encourages them to be watchful as these events unfold. As we review these "riddles" through a spiritual lens, we know that they are simply God's way of letting us know that, through suffering, there is great triumph because of Jesus' death and resurrection.

• What do the parables in Matthew 25 teach you about God's kingdom?

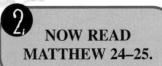

2 NOW READ MATTHEW 24–25.

③ Switchback

Wake up! The Scriptures warn us that we cannot afford to go to sleep, that we must keep watchful because we do not know when Jesus will return. Being watchful means keeping ourselves spiritually alert. The five foolish virgins, the man who buries his talent, and those who miss opportunities to express grace through their treatment of others are examples of falling asleep on the job. Believing is more than lip service. True belief is expressed in how we live—filling our lamps with love; using the gifts and talents God has given us; and sharing grace through feeding the hungry, clothing the naked, visiting prisoners, and welcoming strangers.

• What is the oil in the lamp (25:4)?

Road Sign
• **talent:** In Bible times this was about 75 pounds of gold, equivalent to 20 years of wages for a day laborer.

• In what ways do you stay spiritually alert?

 This week's readings feature several of Jesus' parables. With your team, list each parable (chapters 21–28) and its intended message. Then take a quiz at *amazingbiblerace.com* to see what you've learned.

④ Prayer

O Lord, keep me spiritually alert and prepared for your coming. Reveal to me ways that I may live out your grace in your world. Amen.

His Final Days
Matthew 26

1 Scouting the Terrain

A lot goes on in the days leading up to Jesus' death. A woman anoints Jesus with ointment, Judas negotiates payment for his betrayal of Jesus, and Jesus eats the Passover meal with his disciples. In the middle of dinner, he announces that someone will betray him; and all of the disciples deny it. Peter commits to remain loyal to Jesus, regardless of the circumstances; Jesus responds that Peter will deny him three times before the rooster crows.

As the blood of the lamb protected the Israelites from the last deadly plague in Egypt, Jesus' blood protects all humankind from sin, and points the way to eternal life with God.

The biggest preparation Jesus makes before his death is to pray. From his birth to his death, Jesus shows us how to face suffering and how to handle our enemies—pray! The disciples again show their human limitations as they fall asleep when Jesus asks them to stay awake and pray.

• Why is prayer so important to get us through suffering?

Trailblazers

- Jesus
- the disciples
- chief priests and elders of the people
- Caiaphas
- Simon the leper
- a woman with alabaster jar of ointment
- Judas
- Peter
- a servant girl

2 NOW READ MATTHEW 26.

③ Switchback

The disciples' actions during these final days with Jesus speak volumes to our human tendencies. One of the inner circle, Judas Iscariot, sells out Jesus. What could perhaps be described as the most important prayer the disciples could ever pray is the very one that the disciples fall asleep during. Peter denies he ever knew Jesus.

How quickly our affections shift! Depending on our emotions, our fears, peer pressure, or any number of other factors, we're likely to do and say things that we would otherwise never dream of.

Fortunately, Jesus' plan is bigger than our sinful tendencies. His work on the cross is finished. He triumphed over death. When we trust in Jesus, all of our sins—even those actions mimicking the disciples' actions during Jesus' final days—are forgiven.

• How do you deny Jesus?

• How important is prayer to you? Describe a time when you have persevered to pray even when you were sleepy or uncomfortable.

fast forward The Passion Play, a dramatic portrayal of Christ's final days and hours, is a centuries-old Christian tradition. Write your own Passion Play based on Matthew 21–27. Make a video of your play and upload it to *amazingbiblerace.com* for points.

Or watch a movie version of Christ's passion. (If you watch the popular 2004 movie *The Passion of the Christ,* you will need your parents' permission. This film is a graphic portrayal of Christ's last hours and is rated R.) On your race blog, for points, compare the film to Matthew's account of Jesus' passion.

④ Prayer

Suffering Jesus, forgive me for denying you. Equip me to watch and pray. Amen.

Obedient to Death
Matthew 27

1 Scouting the Terrain

The high priests are determined to have Jesus crucified; so they ultimately present Jesus before Pilate, the governor, who renders final judgment on Jesus. Less than a week earlier, a crowd had yelled, "Hosanna!" as Jesus rode into town. Now a crowd is now yelling to have Jesus crucified.

Jesus does not respond to the allegations or make any attempts to prove his innocence. Jesus quietly and humbly fulfills his mission.

The road to the cross is filled with torment and human degradation. This same man that had healed the sick is bleeding and broken as an African man carries his cross to Golgotha.

• Why, do you think, does God allow Jesus to experience this suffering, the beatings, and the crown of thorns?

Trailblazers

• Jesus
• Judas
• chief priests, elders, and scribes
• Pontius Pilate
• Barabbas
• the crowd
• the governor's soldiers
• Simon
• Mary Magdalene, Mary the mother of James and Joseph, the mother of Zebedee's sons, many other women
• Joseph of Arimathea
• the guard at the tomb

2 NOW READ MATTHEW 27.

3 Switchback

At any moment, Jesus could have stopped his crucifixion. What does it mean to you that he did not?

While our mission can never compare to his, Scripture says that we are to emulate Jesus in attitude and deed. Philippians 2:5-11 speaks of Christ as being a servant, being humbled, and being obedient to death.

Reading the account of Jesus' abuse and agonizing death highlights the importance of what he did for us. Jesus completed his mission in humility. Jesus endured God's wrath so that we wouldn't have to. Jesus submitted to the torture that awaited him.

Praise Jesus for his work on the cross!

• Why, do you think, is Jesus' suffering necessary for the redemption of believers?

• Meditate on what Christ endured so that you could spend eternity with him. Describe your thoughts below.

Road Signs

• **gall:** This can refer to several bitter herbs. The offer of galled wine was torture. Jesus was very thirsty, but the gall made the wine undrinkable.
• **Mary the mother of James and Joseph:** This is possibly Jesus's mother and brothers. Joseph is sometimes called Joses (Mark 15:40).

4 Prayer

Glorious God, thank you for sending your Son to redeem me. Amen.

He Lives!
Matthew 28

1 Scouting the Terrain

Mary Magdalene is a prominent woman featured throughout Jesus' ministry. Though tradition says that Mary was a prostitute, Scripture does not support this belief. But the Bible does tell us that Mary's life was one conversion and change and that Jesus had cleansed her from possession by seven demons. From that point forward, she had been devoted to Christ. Mary follows Jesus during the course of his suffering. She is an onlooker at the trial and is present as Jesus hangs on the cross. She is also a part of the entourage present at Jesus' burial. How appropriate that Mary Magdalene be the first woman used by God to preach the good news: Jesus lives!

Trailblazers

- Jesus
- Mary Magdalene
- the other Mary
- an angel of the Lord
- the guards
- the disciples
- chief priests and elders

- What, do you think, is significant about Mary Magdalene's role in the story of Jesus' death and resurrection?

- Why, do you think, is Mary not surprised to see the angel?

2 NOW READ MATTHEW 28.

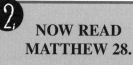

3 Switchback

After his resurrection, Jesus meets the disciples. He gives them the Great Commission, to make disciples of all nations and baptize. During Jesus' brief stay with the disciples, Jesus had prepared the disciples to fulfill this commission. They had been trained to share grace and mercy with others, saving souls, not with their own authority, but with the authority given to them by the Holy Spirit because of Christ's Resurrection. Some of the disciples believed, and some doubted (28:17); but Jesus commissioned all of them.

In the same way, Jesus has commissioned all of us to go into the world and make disciples. We don't have to be members of the clergy to fulfill this role. We don't have to confine our efforts to our local churches. Jesus wants us to go everywhere and tell everyone the Good News.

• Why, do you think, do we need heavenly power to make disciples and baptize?

• How does our congregation obey the Great Commission?

4 Prayer

O Lord, let us operate with a whole mind of faith so that, like Mary Magdalene, we can go and tell others that we serve the Resurrected Savior. Amen.

Water Break

Good work! You've completed the first of the Gospels, the Book of Matthew. For a slightly different take on Jesus' life, keep reading.

Through the Roof
Mark 1–2

1 Scouting the Terrain

Unlike the other Synoptic Gospels, Mark does not contain Jesus' birth story. The Book of Mark begins immediately with John the Baptist's cry of repentance and Jesus' baptism. The opening chapters of Mark highlight Jesus' miraculous healings and exorcisms and the calling of Jesus' first disciples. He speaks and acts with authority, and as his popularity increases, criticism of his work also increases.

• Why might Mark have decided to begin his Gospel with John the Baptist and Jesus' baptism rather than with Jesus' birth?

Trailblazers

• Jesus
• John the Baptist
• Satan
• Simon
• Andrew
• James, son of Zebedee
• John, brother of James
• Simon's mother-in-law
• a man with leprosy
• a paralyzed man and his four friends
• teachers of the Law
• the crowd
• Levi

• Why, do you think, did the disciples quit their jobs to follow Jesus? What does their story say about the economic stakes involved in being follower of Jesus?

2 NOW READ MARK 1–2.

3 Switchback

Can you believe that the paralyzed man's friends were so eager, so desperate, and so courageous that they came up with such a clever plan to get their friend to Jesus? The men cut a hole in the roof of the house then lowered the man on his bed through the roof to Jesus. The group desires Jesus's healing so much that they work to get their friend to him by any means. According to Jesus, this was the picture of faith. After lowering their friend through the roof of the house, Jesus forgives the paralyzed man of his sins before, ultimately, restoring the man's ability to walk.

Jesus is constantly ours. Our access to him is not hindered. We don't have to climb past obstacles to get to him.

• How much do you desire Jesus? What gets in the way of your coming to him?

• When have you wanted Jesus' presence so badly that you would have climbed through a roof to get to him?

Road Signs

• **"removed the roof... and ... having dug through it"** (2:4): This was possible because roofs were flat and made of branches and hardened clay.
• **Synoptic:** This means presenting or having the same view. In this case it refers to the first three Gospels of the New Testament.

In this week's readings, Jesus drives out many evil spirits, unclean spirits, and demons from various individuals. Make a list of each miracle and note the details. Then take a quiz at *amazingbiblerace.com* to check your research and to see what you've learned.

4 Prayer

Dear God, please help me keep me from putting obstacles in the way of coming to you. Amen.

Gotcha!—Not ...
Mark 3

1 Scouting the Terrain

Jesus performed many miracles under pressure. Everywhere he went, Pharisees were lurking to see what part of the Law he would break. They didn't know quite what to make of this guy. They were eager, though, to catch him doing something wrong. Some Pharisees witness Jesus' healing on the sabbath and are quick to begin plotting his murder. As in Matthew, the Pharisees are so detail oriented that they miss the big picture and fail to recognize who Jesus is.

Trailblazers

- Jesus
- the man with a shriveled hand
- Pharisees
- Herodians
- the disciples
- the crowd
- Jesus' mother and brothers

• Why, do you think, were these Pharisees so concerned about Jesus healing on the sabbath?

• Why might Pharisees have felt threatened by Jesus?

2 NOW READ MARK 3.

3 Switchback

Despite the opposition from the those in charge, Jesus' ministry is becoming quite popular. As he travels, his following swells. Jesus is so overwhelmed that he has to find peace and quiet on a small boat.

What's a popular cause today? Many celebrities—actors, athletes, musicians, and politicians, among others—are followed and watched as Jesus was. We love to watch news reports about them, read about them in magazines, and look at pictures of them on the Internet. Surely if we gave as much attention to Christ as we typically give to celebrities, our hearts, our families, and our culture would be radically transformed.

• How much time and energy do you devote to keeping up with your favorite celebrities?

• How much time and energy do you devote to Christ? In what ways do you devote yourself to Christ?

Road Sign

• **Herodians:** This was a non-religious political group that supported the Herodian dynasty. This group collaborated with Rome.

4 Prayer

Lord, give me a renewed excitement for what it means to follow you. Amen.

Peace! Be Still!
Mark 4

1 Scouting the Terrain

Jesus tells three parables (simple stories about everyday people and things that convey a larger truth) concerning the kingdom of God: the parable of the sower, the parable of the scattered seed, and the parable of the mustard seed. These parables concerning seeds tell us that, for our relationship with Christ to remain stable, we must be rooted in the Word of God. Once the relationship has taken root, it will flourish. These parables teach that only fertile, willing vessels holding God's Word will live.

• Why, do you think, did Jesus speak to the public in parables and explain them to his disciples in private?

Trailblazers
• Jesus
• the crowd
• the disciples

• How do we become fertile soil for the Word of God?

2 NOW READ MARK 4.

③ Switchback

The disciples were quite frightened and rather agitated with Jesus. Jesus slept while they worried that their boat would capsize in the storm and they would all drown.

Aren't we like the disciples? Although they have quit their jobs, followed Jesus without question, and witnessed him heal people and rebuke demons, they still lack faith. Storms will always come into our lives unexpectedly. We respond with fear, worry, and anxiety. Then we cry out to God, wondering when relief will come.

Jesus calmed the raging sea. Won't he protect, guard, and love you?

- What do you think about the disciples' reaction? Do you think they understand yet who Jesus is?

- What is faith? Does having faith mean not being concerned about anything?

Visit a grain farmer or find an agriculture specialist who can speak about growing grain. Using the Mark 4 parables about seeds, interview the so that you can gain a greater understanding of Jesus' teaching. After your interview, choose one parable to rewrite, offering an detailed explanation of what Jesus' words really mean. Then have your team act out your parable. Upload videos of your interviews and skits at *amazingbiblerace.com* for points.

④ Prayer

Dear God, strengthen me through the storms of my life. Allow me to feel your divine presence and experience faith that lets me know that you have the power to protect me. Amen.

A Simple Touch
Mark 5–6

WEEK
4
◆
DAY
4

1 Scouting the Terrain

Jesus crosses the Sea of Galilee to heal a demon-possessed man in the country of the Gerasenes. Then he cross the lake again to find a dying 12-year-old girl and a woman who has been bleeding for 12 years. Jairus, the father of the girl and a rich man and synagogue leader, has no problem penetrating the crowd; but the poor bleeding woman, who has spent all her money on physicians has only the opportunity to touch the tassels hanging from Jesus' robe.

Unlike the crowd and his disciples, Jesus is interested in this poor woman. When she touches Jesus's clothes, her bleeding stops immediately. The woman, whose condition made her unclean, risks breaking Levitical codes. (See Leviticus 15:19-30.)

Jesus searches the crowd and calls the woman to testify to the power of faith over disease. After her disclosure, Jesus calls her "daughter."

Meanwhile, Jairus waits patiently on Jesus. Others try to convince him to give up on his daughter, saying that she is dead. Jesus urges him to only believe. Because of the faith of Jairus, his daughter rises from the dead.

• Why does Jesus delay his trip to speak with the sick woman?

Trailblazers

• Jesus
• man with an unclean spirit
• the crowd
• Jairus and his daughter
• woman suffering from hemorrhages
• Peter, James, and John
• the other disciples
• King Herod
• John the Baptist
• Herodias and her daughter

2 NOW READ MARK 5–6.

3 Switchback

Like the friends of the paralyzed man a few chapters back, the woman with the hemorrhage possesses great courage and determination. She risks much to simply touch Christ's clothing. Her faith is so solid that she knows the power that must reside even in the edge of his robe.

Our illnesses—both literally and figuratively—may not be as dramatic as having bled for twelve years. We all will, however, benefit from the tiniest glimpse and touch of Christ. Our souls are certainly sick enough that even a taste of Christ is healing. A brush with his goodness and mercy is soothing. The touch of his robe contains transforming power.

The sick woman, as well as Jairus, believes Christ is who he says he is. Jairus is content to wait on Jesus and he chooses to believe Christ, rather than his mistaken friends.

• When have you listened to voices other than Christ's? What did that do to your faith?

4 Prayer

Lord, increase my faith so that I can know that there is enough power in your garment to make me whole if I just believe. Amen.

But It's Tradition
Mark 7

1. Scouting the Terrain

In their never-ending quest to catch Jesus and his disciples at Law-breaking, some Pharisees catch them eating with unwashed hands. A ceremonial washing was tradition among the elders. These Pharisees are quick to call Jesus on this matter. Jesus, however, turns their empty traditions upside-down. He proclaims that they have let go of God's commands and are clinging to the traditions of men, just as Isaiah prophesied.

Jesus' teaching quickly connects to the status of the heart. He points out that nothing outside one's body can make a person "unclean." Just the opposite is true, he says. The "unclean" things are inside and spill out.

• What is the purpose of religious rituals?

Trailblazers

- Jesus
- Pharisees
- scribes
- the disciples
- a Syrophoenician woman and her daughter
- a deaf and mute man

• What, do you think, does Jesus mean when he speaks of the "unclean" things coming out of a person?

2. NOW READ MARK 7.

3 Switchback

Many traditions in our culture center around family celebrations and holidays—Christmas Eve dinner at Grandma's house, Thanksgiving Day football games with Uncle Jerry, barbeque and fireworks to celebrate the Independence Day. Churches have traditions, too, whether it's a special benediction sung at the end of the worship service or support of a favorite mission or organization.

Traditions help us honor meaningful times, places, and people in our lives. Traditions in our worship service help us see and savor God's grace and mercy.

The Pharisees, however, were so hung up on doing it *only this way*, that they could not understand or appreciate the sentiment behind the traditions.

• What are some of your favorite family or church traditions? What do these traditions celebrate?

• When do traditions in our culture conflict with God's will?

Water Break

You've read nearly half of the shortest Gospel. Next week you'll witness more miracles and see a vision of the end times.

4 Prayer

God, do not allow worldly rules to constrain me from feeling the fullness of your presence. Amen.

Slow Learners
Mark 8–9

① Scouting the Terrain

The disciples have had front-row seats to the most amazing "show" on earth: Jesus' ministry. They witnessed miracles and healings. Still, they don't quite get it. Their discussion of having no bread (8:4) is still one of material concern. Even though they have seen Jesus feed thousands of people with only a small amount of food, they still doubt that God can provide for the physical needs of 12 men.

Jesus lovingly and patiently reproaches them for their lack of faith and belief. He does not give up on them, but we can witness the frustration in his voice through the many rhetorical questions he asks the disciples.

Trailblazers

- Jesus
- the disciples
- the crowd
- Pharisees
- a blind man
- Peter
- James
- John
- a boy with an evil spirit

• Why, do you think, don't the disciples fully understand the lessons Jesus teaches them?

• Why, do you think, do the disciples lack belief and faith, even after having witnessed all that they have seen?

② NOW READ MARK 8–9.

3 Switchback

Reading about the disciples should be encouraging to all of us. While they were privy to the most important events in history, they still struggled with their sins, fears, and doubts.

As Peter, James, and John experience the Transfiguration on the mountain; the other disciples are below trying to heal a man's son. After coming down from the mountain, Jesus chastises them for their lack of faith, and he reiterates that prayer is the solution to overcoming this stumbling block.

Aren't we much like the disciples down below? We have access to the amazing Christ at all times, but our lack of faith prevents us from fully relying on his power. As Jesus did with the disciples, he will also do with us: love and correct, showing grace and mercy.

• When have fear and doubt hindered your growth in Christ?

Road Sign

• **"take up their cross"** (8:34): This image conveys a willingness to suffer for and with Christ. Condemned prisoners were to carry the crossbar of their own cross to the execution site.

4 Prayer

Dear God, help me believe. Amen.

A Servant's Heart
Mark 10

① Scouting the Terrain

"It's my seat!" "No, it's my seat!" You can almost hear the brothers staking claim to the coveted seats on either side of Jesus for all eternity. James and John are more concerned about their status in God's kingdom than with Jesus' suffering. They had not taken to heart Jesus' teaching on humility and greatness, nor do they understand what they are asking. They want something that Christ cannot give. Jesus explains to them that with these seats at his right and left come great suffering. They say that they are ready for the task. Jesus, however, says that the seats are not for him to assign. Only God the Father has authority over such things.

When the rest of the disciples hear of this request, they are furious with James and John. Jesus turns their opinions of greatness upside-down. He tells them that whoever wants to be great must become a servant, and whoever wants to be first must be slave of all.

• Who are some people who became great by becoming servants?

Trailblazers

• Jesus
• the crowds
• Pharisees
• the rich
  young man
• Peter
• James and
  John
• Bartimaeus

② NOW READ MARK 10.

3 Switchback

Serving others requires much of the servant. True service comes from a attitude of the heart that puts others first. It requires a spirit of humility, compassion, and grace. An authentic servant derives great satisfaction from understanding and meeting others' needs.

Jesus could have come to earth in any way possible. In fact, many people expected the Messiah to be a powerful king or a military leader. Jesus' coming in humility and enduring suffering on behalf of those who love him give us a clear message about the Lord we follow and what is expected of us.

A life of service, humility, and putting others first: It's not always easy, but it's exactly what Jesus did.

• When have you served someone else and felt it especially meaningful?

• Why is humbly serving others so satisfying?

• What keeps you from humbly serving others?

4 Prayer

God, give me a heart of humility, devoted to serving others in your name. Amen.

The Real Thing
Mark 11–12

1 Scouting the Terrain

Mark's emphasis on Jesus' authority is a continuing theme as Jesus enters Jerusalem. He demands a colt, cleanses the Temple, curses a fig tree, makes the fig tree live, and resists the challenge of his authority by the Pharisees. Jesus enters into Jerusalem with a royal welcome, the waving of the palms and the shouts of "Hosanna!" We witness a meek and mild Jesus on the donkey, and we witness an angry and infuriated Jesus in the Temple. Jesus' reaction to the sellers in the Temple does not make him any friends; it creates financial problems.

Just before he cleanses the Temple, Jesus curses a fig tree. This incident is symbolic. Jesus curses the fig tree for being impressive but fruitless. By doing so, he is criticizing people and institutions that project power or prestige or righteousness but whose attitudes and behaviors fall short of what God desires.

Trailblazers

- Jesus
- the disciples
- chief priests and teachers of the Law
- Peter
- Herodians
- Sadducees
- the crowd
- a poor widow

• What, do you think, gave Jesus the right to kill the fig tree or to cleanse the Temple?

• What does he accomplish by doing these things?

2 NOW READ MARK 11–12.

52

3 Switchback

Is there any bigger disappointment than realizing that something or someone isn't all that it's cracked up to be? Jesus is hungry and seeks food from a fig tree. Seeing impressive greenery on the plant, he assumes that fruit is there as well. The plant, however, has no fruit, just impressive and deceptive foliage.

This is a sober reminder to followers of Christ that authenticity is important. God knows the sincerity of hearts. Like the Pharisees who opposed Jesus, we can easily fall into the trap of going through the motions or clinging to rituals. Christ reminds us, though, that fancy outward showings have nothing to do with an authentic faith that produces healthy fruit.

- What fruit of sincere faith do you see in your own life? What fruit of the sinful nature do you see in your own life? (Use Galatians 5:16-26 as a reference.)

Road Signs

- **Hosanna:** This word means, "Save [us]!" The crowd was shouting phrases from Psalm 118.
- **"give to the emperor"** (12:17): Even though the Roman taxation and governmental systems were corrupt and unjust in many ways, Jesus nonetheless said not to withhold tax money.
- **two small copper coins:** These coins were called *leptons*. The lepton was the smallest denomination of currency in circulation.

4 Prayer

God, give me an authentic faith so that I bear fruit for you. Amen.

Get Ready!
Mark 13–14

① Scouting the Terrain

Trailblazers

- Jesus
- the disciples, including Peter, James, John, and Andrew
- Simon the leper
- a woman who anoints Jesus
- Judas Iscariot
- chief priests

Jesus urges his disciples to keep an eye on the Pharisees and scribes. But most important, he warns them to keep alert to the signs of the times. These eschatological passages still have relevancy for us today. Mark 13 suggests that Jesus' return will be immediate; however, we are still waiting for the fulfillment of God's plan.

Although we do not know the day nor the hour, we can be prepared. Jesus tells a parable about a master who doesn't give the time of his return. In doing so, his servants and doorkeeper obey the master's commands because he might be home at anytime. We stay ready by doing the work of God's kingdom here and now.

- How are we to live until Christ's return?

WEEK
5
◈
DAY
4

② NOW READ MARK 13–14.

3 Switchback

Prophesying about the destruction of the Temple is no small matter. Jesus is talking about the center of the Jewish world—a magnificent structure of marble and gold that had undergone a major renovation only a few decades earlier—being torn down.

On its surface this prophecy sounds very disturbing. But the destruction of the Temple is part of a larger pattern of death and rebirth. God has something greater in store, something that we will experience when the Son of Man comes in "power and glory" (13:26). Our job is to stay alert.

• What catastrophic events have made you question whether God is in control?

• How can we be sure that God has something better in store for creation?

Road Signs

• **alabaster:** This is a type of marble that was used to make luxurious ointment jars.
• **nard:** This was a rare perfume.
• **eschatological:** This is a term scholars use to refer to beliefs concerning death, the end of the world, or the ultimate destiny of humankind, especially any of various Christian doctrines concerning the Second Coming, the resurrection of the dead, or the Last Judgment.

4 Prayer

Dear God, may I never set my affections too deeply on the things of this world. Prepare me for your return. Amen.

Breathed His Last
Mark 15–16

1 Scouting the Terrain

Jesus' final hours and his resurrection are described as quite spectacular. Accompanying his death are unprecedented events in the physical realm as well as in the spiritual realm. The entire land is put into a darkness for three hours in the middle of the day. The "curtain of the temple" (15:38)—possibly a veil that covered the Temple's innermost and holiest chamber—is torn in two.

Although Jesus is buried in a secure tomb, with a very large stone blocking the entrance, Jesus rises from the dead and leaves the tomb. He then walks and talks again on this earth, appearing to many persons.

- How did the world change when the risen Jesus emerged from the tomb?

Trailblazers

- Jesus
- the disciples
- Pontius Pilate
- Barabbas
- the crowd
- soldiers
- Simon of Cyrene
- chief priests, elders and scribes
- Mary Magdalene; Mary the mother of James and Joses; Salome; and many other women
- Joseph of Arimathea
- a centurion

WEEK
5
◆
DAY
5

Myrrh was an expensive spice and figures prominently in the life and death of Jesus. Follow this spice's use from his birth to his death, noting Matthew 2, Mark 15, and John 19. Then take a quiz at *amazingbiblerace.com* to see what you've learned.

2 NOW READ MARK 15–16.

3 Switchback

Can you even imagine the one-of-kind experience of witnessing the crucifixion, death, burial, and resurrection of Jesus? Certainly, those who loved him were emotionally distraught. With all of the incredible events that were going on too, maybe they were frightened as to what would happen next. Maybe they took an "I told you so" stance toward the doubters. Maybe they themselves doubted that Jesus could overcome such brutality.

Today we have the greatest testimony of the power of Christ: the Bible. We are secure in our future because our future is in this amazing Christ. There's no need to doubt and every reason to tell others of the love of Christ. Heed the call: "Go into all the world and proclaim the good news to the whole creation" (16:15).

• What event surrounding the crucifixion, death, burial, and resurrection of Christ do you find most spectacular? How does meditating on it affect your own faith experience?

Road Signs

• **Cyrene:** This was an important city in North Africa.
• **wine mixed with myrrh** (15:23): This was possibly a primitive painkiller.
• **sour wine:** This offering was made to prolong Jesus' suffering not alleviate it.
• **anoint:** It can be a sacred rite, involving applying oil, to show that someone is chosen to lead. In this case, the anointment was a way of showing affection for the deceased. It is not the same as embalming.

4 Prayer

Thank you, Lord, for your sacrifice on Calvary. Amen.

Water Break

Two down, two to go. You've completed another Gospel. Luke's account is next. Keep going, even though it may feel a little bit like "déjà vu all over again." You're doing a great job!

A Tale of Two Women
Luke 1–5

1 Scouting the Terrain

Luke's Gospel account begins with two pregnant women: Elizabeth and Mary. Theirs are divine pregnancies, announced by the angel Gabriel. Elizabeth becomes pregnant, despite being very old. Mary becomes pregnant despite being a virgin. Elizabeth gives birth to John, the messenger who will prepare the way for the Messiah. Mary gives birth to the Messiah himself.

Zechariah, Elizabeth's husband and John's father, is so taken aback by the news that his elderly wife will have a child that he questions Gabriel. Because of Zechariah's unbelief, the angel deprives of his ability to speak. He stays mute throughout Elizabeth's pregnancy. The couple obeys the angel's mandate to name their child "John" (instead of giving him a family name). Zechariah's obedience miraculously restores his speech, and he sings a beautiful song of hope.

• Look at the songs of Mary (1:46-56) and Zechariah (1:68-79). About whom and what are they singing?

Trailblazers

• Zechariah
• Elizabeth
• Gabriel
• Mary
• John the Baptist
• Joseph
• shepherds
• Baby Jesus
• Simeon
• Anna
• Herod
• Satan
• a man with a spirit of a demon
• Simon
• Simon's mother-in-law

2 NOW READ LUKE 1–5.

③ Switchback

What must Mary have been experiencing when she found out she was pregnant with the Son of God? Fear? Worry? Anxiety? Maybe she was already nauseated with morning sickness. She was probably tired, and maybe her back hurt.

Despite the challenges of pregnancy and the incredible task that God has given her, Mary chooses to praise and trust in the Lord. She obviously knows God's character and past deeds. She praises the Lord with a beautiful song, affirming God's power, mercy, and help. In doing so, she also affirms God has given these gifts to her and her unborn child.

- Why, do you think, does Mary choose to praise God, despite her difficult circumstances of this unexpected pregnancy?

- How are the praise songs we sing in worship similar to or different than Mary's song of praise?

Road Sign

- **Gabriel:** The angel's name means "man of God." Gabriel is one of only two angels called by name in Scripture. The other is Michael.

Luke

 Using all four Gospels and a concordance (and a Bible dictionary if possible), research the 12 apostles chosen by Jesus. With your team, list each man and what you know about him from the Scriptures. Then take a quiz at *amazingbiblerace.com* to find out what you've learned.

④ Prayer

How excellent are your promises, O Lord! We don't always understand them, and sometimes we doubt. Please help our unbelief. Amen.

Judge Not
Luke 6–7

1 Scouting the Terrain

Jesus is always concerned with authenticity. In today's reading, he condemns hypocrisy. He despises when persons point out the sins of others, especially when they engage in those same sins. This does not mean that we should ignore the evil actions of others. On the contrary, Jesus wants us to stand up for truth and against ungodly things. But if we aren't addressing our own sins, any stand we take will be hypocritical and meaningless.

We see this lesson at work when Jesus is eating dinner at the home of Simon, a Pharisee. While they are eating, an unnamed sinful woman comes in, falls at Jesus' feet, washes his feet with her tears, and anoints his feet with ointment. When Simon objects, Jesus explains that this woman, unlike the righteous Pharisee, has great faith because she has come to terms with her sin and thrown herself at Jesus' feet in the hope of being forgiven.

True forgiveness comes from a heart full of mercy and repentance. We don't earn our forgiveness; but one who is forgiven, repents and will forgive others.

Trailblazers

- Jesus
- the disciples
- Pharisees and scribes
- the crowd
- a centurion's servant
- a widow's son at Nain
- John the Baptist
- Simon the Pharisee
- a sinful woman

• What is difficult about confessing and repenting of your sins?

• What, in your opinion, is the hardest part about accepting forgiveness? about offering forgiveness?

2 NOW READ LUKE 6–7.

3 Switchback

Nursing a grudge is easy. You might feel that you're entitled to stay angry with a friend or sibling who has wronged you. "You have every right to be angry with her," someone might say. And you totally agree.

Jesus denounces this line of thinking. We are to forgive others. We are to love them with the love of Christ. We are to offer grace, help, and mercy. We are to be peacemakers not hostile revenge-seekers.

Revenge feels good because we humans, by nature, are self-serving, self-preserving, and self-focused. We want payback for however we have been wronged. But just think of Jesus: He died for those who were once his enemies and did not bear a grudge. By his death, he gives love, forgiveness, and freedom to those who trust in him.

Let us be agents of Christ to our enemies.

• Why, do you think, is it difficult to love our enemies?

• Describe a time you chose to reject revenge and embrace forgiveness. What was that like?

4 Prayer

Jesus, thanks for forgiving my sins. Help me remember that I am a forgiven forgiver. Amen.

Let It Shine
Luke 8-9

① Scouting the Terrain

Jesus uses parables to make spiritual matters plain in the simple minds of humans. He draws an analogy likening people to the environments upon which seed might fall. The seed symbolizes God's Word.

He also talks about putting one's lamp on a lampstand so that those who enter may see the light. Jesus' teachings are not to be hidden or put away. They are truth that is meant to shine, to illuminate the darkness in this world, to glow brightly for all to see.

Today's reading continues with several of Jesus' miracles, as he feeds the five thousand, drives out demons, and quiets the raging sea.

• Why does Jesus command his followers to let their lamps shine?

• What will happen when Jesus' lamps are shining brilliantly in our world?

Trailblazers

- Jesus
- the disciples
- Mary Magdalene, Joanna, Susanna, and many other women
- the crowd
- Jesus' mother and brothers
- Gerasene demoniac
- Jairus and his daughter
- Herod
- Moses
- Elijah
- a boy with a demon
- three persons on the road

② NOW READ LUKE 8-9.

3 Switchback

It's not always easy to tell others about Jesus. Sometimes we'd rather keep our faith to ourselves to avoid conflict or ridicule. Sometimes we don't feel confident in our Bible knowledge. Maybe we have our own doubts and just aren't sure what we believe.

Being a witness for Christ is an ongoing process. Jesus wants you to be a light for him. Anything that he has called you to do, he will also equip you to do. Jesus himself will help you learn more, grow in faith, and feel confident in your expression of it. So many people in our world, in your city, in your school, in your neighborhood, need the love and light of Christ. Be a glaring beacon for him. Don't hide your light under a jar.

• What are some ways you can be the light of Jesus to a lost and dying world?

• What is it that most prevents you from being the light of Christ?

Road Sign

• **jar:** Biblical jars were made of pottery, so light couldn't shine through them the way light can through our glass jars.

Luke

4 Prayer

Dear Lord, we are grateful for the ability to be sent out by you. Please equip us with your spirit so that we might maximize our potential as workers for your kingdom. Amen.

Surprise Ending
Luke 10–11

1 Scouting the Terrain

Jesus tells the parable of the Good Samaritan to an expert of the Law to illustrate what he means by the word *neighbor*. Jesus presents a scenario to the man in which a person is beaten, robbed and left to die. A priest and a Levite (someone from the priestly tribe of Levi who served at the Temple) both passed by the man without helping him. Jesus doesn't say why they passed by. Maybe they were short on time; maybe they were concerned that, were the beaten man to die, contact with a corpse would make them ritually unclean.

Then a Samaritan passes by, shows compassion, and helps the man. Jews and Samaritans have a common ancestry; but because they disagreed about legal matters and how to properly worship God, the two groups despised each other. For Jesus, a Jew, to tell a story to his Jewish audience in which the hero is a Samaritan is truly remarkable.

Trailblazers

- Jesus
- 70 persons
- the disciples
- a lawyer
- Martha
- Mary
- a woman in the crowd
- the crowd
- Pharisees, lawyers, and scribes

WEEK
6
◆
DAY
4

- What does the parable of the good Samaritan tell us about what it means to love our neighbors?

2 NOW READ LUKE 10–11.

3 Switchback

Jesus commands his followers to be in relationship, rather than in religion, with him.

Being a Christian means more than simply following the doctrines, rituals, and methods of the church. Jesus desires for us to be his witnesses—not just on Sunday but every day of the week. He desires for us to reach out to people from racial backgrounds other than our own.

It's easy to stay in your comfort zone and help people who are just like you. Reaching across lines of race, ethnicity, political persuasion, and religious identity is much more difficult. But God calls all of us to follow the good Samaritan's example by getting out of our little "holy huddles" and offer the love and help of Christ to others.

• What is stopping you from being a "good Samaritan" to those who aren't just like you?

• When have you ministered to or worshiped with people of another cultural background? Describe that experience.

Road Sign

• **Samaritan:** This term refers to a religious group who claims to be the remnant of the lost tribes of Israel. Ancient Samaritans believed that Mt. Gerizim, not Jerusalem, was the proper place to worship God. This belief, along with other factors put the Samaritans at odds with their Jewish neighbors.

Luke

Get out of your comfort zone and find a ministry that serves persons very different from you in terms of race, ethnicity, or age. Work with this ministry for 6 months. Keep a video diary of your work and upload it at *amazingbiblerace.com*. Your team must also upload a scan or photo of a team "covenant," in which everyone agrees to serve in this capacity for 6 months, to receive full points.

4 Prayer

Lord, give us unity as Christians. Help us to commit to your will as a team effort.
  Amen.

Don't Worry. Be Happy!
Luke 12–14

1 Scouting the Terrain

Trailblazers

- Jesus
- the crowd
- the disciples
- a crippled woman
- Pharisees, lawyers, and scribes
- a man with dropsy
- dinner guests
- tax collectors and other sinners

Jesus both warns and encourages his followers. He warns against the hypocritical activities inspired and led by Pharisees. And he assures his followers that they should not fear these Pharisees, for Pharisees do not have the authority to condemn. We should only fear the One who has authority over all things.

While attending a dinner party at a prominent Pharisee's house, Jesus teaches an important lesson on humility. Jesus says that we should not give ourselves promotions, exaltations, and other accolades. He states that everyone who lifts himself up will be brought down, but the one who humbles himself or herself will be exalted.

Finally, Jesus reminds his disciples that there is a cost to following him: Anyone who follows Christ must take up his or her cross daily.

- Why, do you think, does Jesus tell his followers not to worry? What other passages about worry can you find in the Bible?

- What, do you think, does it mean to be humble before God?

2 NOW READ LUKE 12–14.

3 Switchback

Much profound truth is embedded in that perky, if slightly annoying, 1988 Bobby McFerrin tune "Don't Worry. Be Happy." Jesus commands the disciples to stop worrying and reminds them of God's power and and grace and character. Christians have the assurance that God will, in fact, take care of our every need and will come to our rescue at the appropriate time.

Overcoming worry requires consistent faith and diligence in prayer. A compulsive worrier cannot expect to overcome his or her anxiety overnight; but in due time, with constant prayer and faith, one can achieve true peace of mind.

• Are you a worrier? Why, or why not?

• If you are a worrier, what do you need to stop worrying about?

Luke

4 Prayer

Jesus, take away my worries. Amen.

Road Sign

• **dropsy:** A person with this disease is swollen with fluid accumulated in the cavities of his or her body. Nowadays, we call it edema.

Water Break

In the first half of Luke, you read some of the Bible's most memorable stories. In the second half, you'll read a lot more parables and take yet another emotional trip through Holy Week.

I Once Was Lost
Luke 15–17

1 Scouting the Terrain

Chapter 15 features the same theme, being lost, in three different parables. Luke uses these three parables to illustrate God's mercy and love for all people. God reveals to humanity that we are all worth the time and energy of an intensive search. Jesus is interested in finding the lost and bringing them into a communal relationship with him. The sacrifices of the shepherd, the woman, and the father reveal Jesus' willingness to sacrifice for those whom he loves.

Trailblazers

- Jesus
- tax collectors and sinners
- Pharisees and scribes
- the disciples
- ten people with leprosy

• In each parable, who (or what) is lost? Who is the seeker? What is the basic message of these parables?

• What, do you think, do these three stories say about sin and grace? How does the attitude of the prodigal son's brother support your answers?

2 NOW READ LUKE 15–17.

3 Switchback

Evidently Jesus knew thousands of years ago what ABC-TV executives know today. The themes of being lost, being searched after, and being found profoundly resonate with people. Just as we can identify with Jack and Kate as they struggle to escape the island on the hit TV show *Lost,* we can also identify with the main characters in Jesus' parables.

We've all misplaced something or lost our way in a store, a large building, a big city, or a dense forest. Locating that lost object or finding your way home is frustrating and takes a lot of time and energy. Depending on the value of the lost object or the level of frustration in finding it, we may choose to stop looking for it.

Today's parables remind us that, before we come to Jesus, we are lost. But we are of such extreme worth to God that we are pursued until we are found and led on the pathway home. God always finds those whom God seeks.

• Why, do you think, does Jesus use the language of "lost and found" to describe our salvation?

Luke

4 Prayer

God, praise you for finding me when I was lost. Thank you that you'll never let me go. Amen.

The Lord He Wanted to See
Luke 18–19

1 Scouting the Terrain

The sharing of wealth is an important focus of Luke's Gospel. The rich young ruler is unwilling to sell his possessions and give the money to the poor so that he can follow Jesus. Zaccheus, the tax collector, however, *is* willing to do it. Zaccheus is a sinner who had exploited people and taken advantage of the poor for the sake of personal gain. Underneath this sinfulness, though, is an inward desire to be in the presence of Jesus. Zaccheus is even willing to climb a tree to get a look at him. Jesus singles out Zaccheus and calls to him; and they have dinner together.

Without any prompting from Jesus, Zaccheus repents and offers to give back to the poor four times what he had taken from them.

• What does Jesus' interaction with Zaccheus say about forgiveness, repentance, God's love for humanity?

Trailblazers

• Jesus
• people and their infants
• the disciples
• a rich ruler
• blind man
• Zaccheus
• the crowd
• Pharisees, chief priests, scribes, and other leaders of the people

• What, do you think, causes Zaccheus to climb a tree to see Jesus?

2 NOW READ LUKE 18–19.

3 Switchback

Have you ever felt ostracized? hated? Have you ever regretted your actions but were unsure how to make amends with God and those you'd hurt?

Be encouraged by Zaccheus. He is despised by his people because he has cheated and hurt them. Zaccheus has made money at the expense of others. Something, however, stirs in his heart. He longs to see Jesus.

After his encounter, he is a changed man. He makes everything right with those people he has wronged, and Jesus declares his salvation.

Jesus changes us. Regardless of how we've hurt others or how reviled we are for what we have done, Jesus will come to our home and lead us to repentance.

• How can you relate to Zaccheus? What can you learn from his story?

Road Sign

• **Tax collector:** Roman officials in Palestine had direct responsibility for collecting regular taxes, such as a poll and land taxes. Private contractors would pay for the right to collect the taxes and tried to make a profit through the transaction. Because many tax collectors were guilty of corruption, tax collecting was a very unpopular profession.

4 Prayer

Lord, show me how I've sinned against others. Change me so that I may repent and make things right. Amen.

Money, Money, Money
Luke 20–22

1 Scouting the Terrain

A poor widow does not go unnoticed by Jesus. As all of the rich are putting their (assumedly large) gifts into the Temple treasury, a woman places two small copper coins. Jesus contrasts her gift with the gifts from the rich. He commends her generosity, saying that she has put in more than all of the others. Perhaps those listening would have been confused at his seeming contradiction. As usual, though, Christ focuses on the state of one's heart and attitude not on outward behaviors.

• What, do you think, motivated the widow to give all she had to live on?

Trailblazers

• Jesus
• chief priests, scribes, and elders
• spies
• Sadducees
• rich people
• a poor widow
• Judas
• the apostles

• Why, do you think, does Jesus say that she has given more than the others?

2 NOW READ LUKE 20–22.

3 Switchback

Money. Acquiring wealth gives us luxury and choices. We need a certain amount of money to make ends meet and pay bills.

Jesus has a lot to say about our relationship with money. We have seen him deal harshly with wealthy people who were not generous with their money. In the poor widow, Jesus sees someone who is very generous. He knows that this woman has given as an offering all that she has to live on.

She could have given only a portion of her money or not given any money at all. How would she meet her basic needs? Despite any reservations she may have had, the widow's obvious love for God and dependence on God are far greater than her love for or dependence on money.

• How would you describe your relationship with money?

Luke

• If you had only $5.00, what would you do with it?

Look at Jesus' teachings about money and service in this week's readings. How would you summarize Jesus' commands about priorities, wealth, power, service, and humility? Go to *amazingbiblerace.com* and take a quiz.

4 Prayer

Merciful God, help me love you and depend on you more than I do on money. Amen.

The Suffering Substitute
Luke 23

1. Scouting the Terrain

Jesus' disciples desert him. Peter denies him. Judas betrays him. An angry mob is yelling that he be put to death.

Human hearts can be so fickle, yet Jesus is constant. While many people, including some of his closest followers, reject Jesus, Jesus embraces them with love. He asks for forgiveness on their behalf. While his body is nailed to a wooden cross, bleeding, broken, and bruised, he listens to the ridicule of a criminal deriding him about his claim of being the Messiah.

Of course, Jesus could have come down from the cross. Instead, he chooses to suffer and die for us. His sacrifice and amazing grace are revealed in Jesus' promise to the other criminal that he would experience paradise with him on this day.

• Why, do you think, did people turn so quickly against Jesus?

• Why, do you think, does Jesus say that the people don't know what they are doing? Why don't they know?

Trailblazers

• Jesus
• Pilate
• Herod and Herod's soldiers
• chief priests, scribes, the leaders, and people
• Barabbas
• Simon of Cyrene
• two criminals
• a centurion
• Joseph of Arimathea
• women

2. NOW READ LUKE 23.

3 Switchback

Meditating on the Crucifixion brings one to a place of mourning. Many of the eyewitnesses were looking for entertainment. Scripture says, however, that their delight turned to grief. In verse 48, they beat their breasts and returned home. Something about the death of Jesus made them sad.

We have a hard time imagining the brutality Christ endured as he died. Focusing on the truth of his death should bring us all to a place of humility and gratitude.

Jesus was a completely innocent and completely righteous substitute for our sins. What an amazing act of mercy!

• How, do you think, does Christ's suffering reveal both his human and divine nature?

• Meditate on Christ's sacrifice on your behalf. Then write about your thoughts.

4 Prayer

Oh Lord, thank you for your completely selfless act of sacrifice.
May I be always humble and always grateful. Amen

Luke

Living and Breathing
Luke 24

1 Scouting the Terrain

The disciples just really can't believe it. They had left their homes to follow Jesus. They had seen him do the miraculous: walking on water, feeding thousands from just a few loaves and fishes, healing the sick, and restoring the dead to life. But this is too much. Could Jesus really be alive after dying a brutal death on the cross?

Jesus is, as always, patient, loving, and compassionate toward the hard-headed disciples. He reappears to them, opens the Scriptures with them, and feeds them as he did before his death. Now their eyes are opened, and their hearts burn. The power of the Word of God is effective in revealing Jesus to blind eyes and hard hearts.

• Why, do you think, don't the disciples believe at first?

Trailblazers

• Jesus
• Mary Magdalene
• Joanna
• Mary the mother of James
• other women
• two men in dazzling clothes
• the apostles
• Cleopas and a companion

• What, do you think, does it take for them to have faith?

2 NOW READ LUKE 24.

3 Switchback

Some Christians have been exposed to Christianity in their homes since before they could talk. Even if you are a new Christian or new to church, you probably can rattle off a few of the major "Sunday school stories." In the church, we create a vocabulary, of sorts, from all of the things we know about Jesus. We're like the disciples in that way. We know Jesus. We know what he says about himself. We know that he's capable of powerful works. Yet we still struggle to believe that he's real, alive, and working in our lives.

Have faith, Christian! Talk to yourself every day about who God is. Our Jesus lives. Our God is working. Our Holy Spirit is changing hearts.

• When have you doubted Jesus' work, even though you know that he's alive?

• What do the "Sunday school stories" you know say about the truth of who God really is?

4 Prayer

Dear Jesus, help me always know your living presence and your life-changing power. Amen.

Water Break

Great work! You've finished Luke's Gospel. John's is the next and final Gospel. You're doing a great job with this leg of the race so far. Keep going!

In the Beginning
John 1

1 Scouting the Terrain

John's Gospel opens with "In the beginning." John wants his readers to understand that Jesus' story goes back to the beginning of time, before creation. John is clear from the get go that Jesus is not just a man who taught and healed and then died on a cross. Rather, Jesus is the Word of God, through whom all of creation came into being.

Trailblazers

- Jesus
- John the Baptist
- Simon Peter
- Andrew
- Philip
- Nathanael

John makes another important claim about Jesus at the beginning of his Gospel: "In [Jesus] was life, and the life was the light of all people" (1:4). Think about light and life. Light emanates from the sun and brings about life by warming our planet and feeding the plants that supply the world with food and oxygen. Likewise God's Word emanates from its source and gives life to everything it touches.

John acknowledges the darkness in the world but assures us that this darkness cannot overcome the light of God's Word. This simple message gives hope to every person who is going through a dark time in life.

• What are some areas of darkness in your life? What are some dark places in our world today?

• In what ways can you reflect the light of Christ in places of darkness?

2 NOW READ JOHN 1.

3 Switchback

The Greek word that John uses to describe Jesus as the Word is *logos*. But *logos* means more than just "word." In Greek philosophy logos is the principle or pattern that gives order to the entire universe. John is suggesting to his audience that Christ had a role in creation; and that, through Christ, God continues to bring order to the universe.

Thus when we study Jesus' life and teaching, we get much more than an example of a wise man who did incredible things: We get a glimpse of God and of the way that God wants us to live.

• What have you learned from Jesus about God and the way that God wants you to live?

• How might your words and actions give others a glimpse of God?

John

4 Prayer

Thank you, God, for living as one of us. Help us to learn from the life of Jesus as we continue this leg of the race and to reflect the light of Christ through our words and actions. Amen.

Road Sign

• **"angels of God ascending and descending"** (1:51): This is a reference to Jacob's dream of a ladder to heaven in Genesis 28:12.

Born Again?
John 2–3

1 Scouting the Terrain

Seeing Jesus at a wedding reception in John 2 is refreshing. It's good to know that Jesus didn't spend all of his time in the synagogue or preaching in the countryside. Jesus also liked to unwind, to socialize, and to have fun. At this particular wedding, Jesus is a big hit, turning water into fine wine after the provided wine had run out.

The story that follows shows a different side of Jesus. While in Jerusalem for the Passover festival, Jesus expresses outrage toward the Temple merchants selling sacrificial animals by turning over the tables of the money changers (those who converted foreign currency into money acceptable at the Temple). You may recall that in the Synoptic Gospels (Matthew, Mark, and Luke), this episode appears toward the end of the story. In John, by contrast, it appears near the beginning.

Trailblazers

• **Jesus**
• **Jesus' mother**
• **Temple merchants**
• **money changers**
• **Nicodemus**
• **John the Baptist**

• In what ways does your congregation promote relaxing, socializing, and having fun? Why are these things important?

• Look at the story of Jesus cleansing the Temple in John (2:13-22) and in Matthew (21:12-17), Mark (11:15-17), and Luke (19:45-46). How are these stories similar? How are they different?

2 NOW READ JOHN 2–3.

3 Switchback

The phrase *born again* has been so central to the Christian faith for so long that most people today don't find it usual at all. But the Pharisee Nicodemus, hearing for the first time Jesus' instruction to be born again, the concept seemed very strange. How can someone emerge from his or her mother's womb a second time? Everything we know about physics and biology won't permit it.

Jesus explains that being born into a new life doesn't require us to spend more time in our mother's bellies. We have been born of the flesh; now we must also be born of the spirit. We do this by surrendering our lives to God and claiming God's gift of salvation through Christ.

• How does a person change when he or she gives over his or her life to God?

• How has your relationship with Christ changed your life? In what ways have you been "born again"?

Road Sign

• **cattle, sheep, and doves:** These were animals sold for sacrifices in the Temple.

4 Prayer

God thank you for the gift of new life. Help us to claim this gift by turning over our lives to you. Amen.

In John, Jesus describes himself in all sorts of creative ways: "the bread of life," "the light of the world," and "the good shepherd" to name just a few. Based on what you know about Jesus from the Gospels, come up with three of your own creative names for Jesus. Then take a quiz on Jesus' identity at *www.amazingbiblerace.com.*

At Jacob's Well
John 4–5

1 Scouting the Terrain

Jews and Samaritans did not get along. There was significant animosity between the two groups over proper worship practices (see 4:20) and cleanliness rituals (see 4:9), among other things. Yet Jesus, a Jew, meets with a Samaritan woman, which is taboo for two reasons: Jews do not mix with Samaritans, and Jewish religious teachers do not mix with women in public. He crosses these boundaries at a location that symbolically links the Jewish and Samaritan traditions: a well established by Jacob, the common ancestor of Jews and Samaritans.

Jacob is most famous for his all-night wrestling match with God. At a spot special to Jacob—the one who struggled with God—the Samaritan woman struggles with Jesus and his religious tradition, the townspeople struggle with whether or not Jesus is the Messiah, and Jesus' disciples struggle with how to act now that Jesus is spending time with women.

Trailblazers

- Jesus
- a Samaritan woman
- a royal official and his son
- a sick man at the Sheep Gate

- With whom do you not get along? The Samaritans and Jews had Jacob in common. What do you have in common with the people with whom you don't belong?

2 NOW READ JOHN 4–5.

3 Switchback

Though the story about the man at the pool of Beth-zatha is only found in John, all four Gospels include stories about Jesus healing on the sabbath (and getting in trouble for it). In this instance, Jesus not only healed the man, but he also instructed the man to "take [his] mat and walk" (verse 8). Carrying a mat was a violation of sabbath law. As in the story of Jesus healing a man with a withered hand (see Mark 3:1-6), religious leaders are so angry about what Jesus has done that they seek to kill him.

• Jesus got in trouble for healing a man. Who are some people in the world today who are ridiculed and attacked for trying to do good things?

• How can you find the courage to do good even when doing the right thing is dangerous or unpopular?

John

Racing Tip

The use of the term "Jews" in John's Gospel has long been a problem for readers, especially because "the Jews" in John are almost always Jesus' adversaries. This negative portrayal of Jews has been used for centuries to justify the persecution of Jewish persons. It's important to note, however, that Jesus and most (if not all) of his closest followers were Jewish and that the vast majority of Jewish people were not hostile toward Jesus. When John writes of "the Jews," he is writing about a small group of Jewish religious leaders, particularly scribes and Pharisees, who oppose Jesus' teaching.

4 Prayer

Lord, open our ears so that we can hear what you are calling us to do. Give us the courage to obey your voice, even when we face ridicule. Amen.

Spiritual and Physical
John 6–7

1 Scouting the Terrain

Trailblazers

- **Jesus**
- **Jesus' disciples**
- **Nicodemus**
- **Jesus' brothers**
- **Pharisees**
- **Temple police**

In all four Gospels, Jesus uses bread imagery to describe who he is and what he has come to do. In Matthew, Mark, and Luke, Jesus famously breaks a loaf of bread the night before his death and says, "Take, eat; this is my body," instituting the ritual we now know as Holy Communion or the Eucharist.

John recounts a much earlier instance of Jesus using bread as a metaphor for his ministry and mission. He compares himself to manna, the bread that came down from heaven to feed the Israelites in the wilderness. (See Exodus 16.) Much as the manna quenched the Israelites' physical hunger and enabled them to lived in the desert, Jesus quenches our spiritual hunger and enables us to have eternal life.

- In what ways is bread an appropriate metaphor for Jesus?

WEEK

8

❖

DAY

4

- When are you most spiritually hungry? In what ways do you quench this hunger?

 Jesus tells us that the "spirit" and not the "flesh" gives us life. (John 6:63). Try a sort of fasting this week as a way to go beyond the "flesh" and focus on the "spirit." Pick something you eat or drink a lot of but don't need and go the entire week without it. Use the cravings you get for that food or beverage, as reminders to spend time in prayer. Blog about your experience or upload a video diary at *www.amazingbiblerace.com*.

2 NOW READ JOHN 6–7.

3 Switchback

As the Pharisees are conspiring to arrest and kill Jesus, Nicodemus, himself a Pharisee, takes a stand. He asks rhetorically, "Our law does not judge people without first giving them a hearing to find out what they are doing, does it?" (7:51). Nicodemus is risking his reputation by sticking up for the teacher who confused him by insisting that he be "born again" (3:1-21). The Pharisees reply by sarcastically suggesting that Nicodemus, like Jesus, must come from Galilee. In other words, Nicodemus must be poor and uneducated. They add, "Search and you will see that no prophet is to arise from Galilee" (7:52).

• Why, do you think, did Nicodemus decide to stand up to the other Pharisees on Jesus' behalf?

• When have you taken a difficult stand for someone or something? What happened?

Extra Mile

Jesus mentions bread a lot in Chapter 6. He uses bread to feed the great crowd and then talks about "bread from heaven" (6:31) and refers to himself as the "bread of life" (6:35, 48). Why bread? Why not lamb of life or rice of life or falafel of life? Take the time to brainstorm a list of as many properties of bread as you can. Then think of how the words used to describe bread also describe Jesus.

4 Prayer

God, we thank you for the courage of Nicodemus and all who stand up for what is right. We ask that you would help us to do the same. Amen.

Some Pretty Big Claims
John 8–9

1 Scouting the Terrain

Throughout the Book of John, Jesus makes some pretty big claims about who he is. In Chapter 8, however, he takes it to a new level. He has already spoken about how close he is to God; but in verse 24, he makes public a statement that he had previously made only to the disciples (see 6:20)—"I am." (Some translations say "It is I" in 6:20 and "I am he" in 8:24, but in both cases the original Greek literally says "I am.")

Trailblazers

- **Jesus**
- **Jesus' disciples**
- **an adulterous woman**
- **Pharisees**
- **a blind man**

"I am" (also translated "I am who I am" or "I will be what I will be") was God's answer to Moses when Moses asked God for the divine name (Exodus 3:14). For Jesus to call himself "I am" is to tell people that he and God are one. Whereas we might say, "I am Steve," or "I am a plumber," God is the only one who can say "I am" and leave it at that.

- Why might some of Jesus' statements have confused or angered the people who first heard them?

WEEK
8
◆
DAY
5

- How can you help people better understand who Jesus is?

Racing Tip

In some translations John 7:53–8:11 is set apart in brackets or italics. This Scripture is missing in the most ancient manuscripts. In other manuscripts, it is found elsewhere in John or even in Luke.

2 NOW READ JOHN 8–9.

3 Switchback

The Pharisees make the audacious claim in 9:31 that God does not listen to sinners. If they believe that, they are forgetting or ignoring much of the Old Testament. Jacob lied to his father, tricked his brother, and stole from his father-in-law; but God nonetheless met with and blessed Jacob. Moses murdered someone, but God called him to lead the Israelites out of Egypt. David had a man killed so that he could marry the man's wife, with whom David had already committed adultery, but God still spoke to David and heard his cries in the Psalms.

Jesus broke all sorts of molds. The Pharisees, no matter how hard they try, cannot figure Jesus out. He does one thing that shows God's favor and power—such as healing the blind man—but he does it on the sabbath which, according to the Pharisees, is contrary to God's will. He claims to be the Messiah, but Jesus escapes the crowds when they want to make him king—the proper role, many of them believed, that a Messiah should play.

• Why is it important for Christians to affirm that God does indeed listen to sinners?

• What boxes do we put around God? What are the dangers of putting limits on who God is or can be?

Water Break

All the bread you've consumed in these opening chapters of John is probably making you thirsty. Relax with a cold drink and get ready for some of the most interesting and exciting chapters in the Gospels.

4 Prayer

God, thank you for listening to me, a sinner. Deliver me from the temptation to place limits on who you are or what you can do. In the name of the great "I am," amen.

Controversy
John 10–11

1 Scouting the Terrain

John 10–11 tells of more instances in which people are angry with Jesus for what he does and says. Jesus teaches that he is the good shepherd and suggests that the religious authorities of the day are, by contrast, bandits and thieves. Jesus goes on to say, "The Father and I are one," a statement that many of his adversaries considered blasphemy—an offense punishable by death. In response to Jesus' bold proclamation, his opponents pick up stones and threaten to kill him.

Controversial statements aren't the only thing that gets Jesus in trouble. Jesus also angers the religious authorities by performing yet another incredible sign. When he raises Lazarus—who had been dead for four days—people are amazed, and the Pharisees' plot to destroy Jesus becomes more urgent.

Trailblazers

• **Jesus**
• **the disciples**
• **Lazarus**
• **Martha**
• **Mary**
• **Pharisees**

• Why, do you think, were some people so offended by Jesus' words and actions?

• Which of Jesus' teachings or acts do you find most difficult or baffling?

Racing Tip

John 11 twice says that Lazarus had been dead for four days (verses 17 and 39). According to ancient Jewish belief, the soul stayed near the body for three days after death, so death was not considered final until the fourth day.

2 NOW READ JOHN 10–11.

3 Switchback

Jesus heals in two different ways in the story of Lazarus. The obvious healing takes place when Jesus raises Lazarus from the dead. The more subtle healing takes place in verse 11:35 when "Jesus began to weep." Miraculously removing Mary and Martha's grief over their brother's death would not have been right—they needed the chance to mourn. Numbing the pain would not do them any good. Instead, Jesus heals by weeping with these sisters.

- When has a close friend cried with you or sat with you when you were having a rough time? How did your friend's presence help you heal?

- Why, do you think, did Jesus wait before going to see Lazarus? Why didn't Jesus travel to Bethany as soon as he learned that Lazarus was ill?

John

Road Signs

- **"festival of the Dedication"** (10:22): This phrase refers to Chanukah.
- **Bethany:** This is a city just east of Jerusalem.

4 Prayer

Good shepherd, lead us through your gates and into your mighty presence. Amen.

When Love Gets Complicated
John 12–14

1 Scouting the Terrain

Today's reading starts out with triumph and joy. The people celebrate Jesus' entry into Jerusalem. The work of the Messiah is about to be done. How this work will be done will surprise many people.

In chapters 12–13 John gives us a glimpse of Jesus' humanity. Jesus says that his "soul is troubled" (12:27) by his imminent death. Later, he expresses hurt that someone close to him will betray him (13:21). In the person of Jesus, God is enduring physical and emotional pain to redeem creation.

Jesus' disciples see that their teacher is upset, but they cannot understand all that is going on, making Jesus' final week all the more lonely and painful.

Trailblazers

- **Jesus**
- **Judas**
- **Peter**
- **Philip**
- **the other disciples**
- **Mary**
- **Martha**
- **Lazarus**
- **Greeks**

• What is comforting about knowing that Jesus experienced human emotions, such as fear and loneliness?

• How does God comfort you during difficult and uncertain times?

2 NOW READ JOHN 12–14.

3 Switchback

Persons about to be executed get to choose their last meal. Anything they want is at their disposal. For Jesus' final meal, he does more than eat: He washes his disciples' feet. Washing feet may not strike you as impressive. Perhaps you have participated in a footwashing during Holy Week worship services, and it wasn't that bad. But we live in a time of shoes, socks, sidewalks, carpeting, automobiles, and indoor plumbing. Jesus, on the other hand, lived in a time of sandals, no socks, dirt roads, dirt floors, lots of walking, and infrequent bathing. The disciples certainly would've had disgusting feet. But Jesus washes them nonetheless. God literally gets down on the floor and scrubs dirty, smelly feet to set an example of the kind of humble, sacrificial love we should show people. (And Jesus didn't even ask his disciples to return the favor!)

• In what ways do people in your congregation show the humble, sacrificial love that Jesus demonstrates in this Scripture?

• How can you humbly serve your friends and family this week? How can you serve enemies and strangers?

John

Road Signs

• **Advocate:** This is a name for the Holy Spirit.
• **"the [disciple] whom Jesus loved"** (13:23): Scripture doesn't tell us the name of the beloved disciple. Traditionally, the church has identified him as John.

Shortly before his death, Jesus tells his disciples about the coming of the Advocate, or Holy Spirit. Reread what Jesus says about the Advocate in John 14–16, and write a short paragraph about who the Holy Spirit is and what the Holy Spirit does. Compare your paragraph with those of your teammates. Then take a quiz about the Holy Spirit at *www.amazingbiblerace.com.*

4 Prayer

Lord, thank you for showing us what it means to love. Help us follow your example by humbly serving others. In your name, amen.

Before I Leave
John 15–17

WEEK
9
◇
DAY
3

1 Scouting the Terrain

Trailblazers
- Jesus
- the disciples

Jesus is preparing his disciples for life after he is gone. He tells them that, after he leaves, "the Advocate" or "Spirit of truth" (better known as the Holy Spirit) will be with them to guide them. These assurances hardly lessen the pain of knowing that Jesus will no longer be with them in the flesh.

Despite the comfort promised by the Holy Spirit, much of Jesus' message is disconcerting. He tells the disciples that the "world hates [them]" and will persecute them, force them out of the synagogues, and kill them (15:18, 20; 16:2). But Jesus assures the disciples that their sorrow will turn to joy, much as the pain of childbirth yields the joy of a newborn baby.

• What are some of the costs of discipleship in today's world?

• What are some of the benefits of being a follower of Christ?

2 NOW READ JOHN 15–17.

3 Switchback

John 17 is one long prayer in which Jesus prays for his disciples, asking God to "protect them" (verse 11) and "sanctify them in the truth" (verse 17). Jesus acknowledges that the disciples will suffer and face persecution and asks that God will watch over them during these trying times.

What makes this prayer so special is that Jesus is not only praying for the 12 men who were by his side during his earthly ministry but also for his followers today. He prays, "I ask not only on behalf of these [the disciples], but also on behalf of those who will believe in me through their word, that they may all be one" (17:20-21).

• What words of comfort do you hear in Jesus' prayer?

• Jesus desires that we "may all be one." How can the church today do a better job of putting our differences aside and uniting as Christ's followers?

Road Sign

• **sanctify:** This means "to make holy."

John

4 Prayer

Lord, long before I was born, you said a prayer on my behalf. Today I pray for all of those disciples who will come after me. Help me pass on your message to these disciples through my words, my actions, and my example. Amen

Death and New Life
John 18–20

1 Scouting the Terrain

Trailblazers

- Jesus
- Annas
- Peter
- Caiaphas
- Pontius Pilate
- Joseph of Arimathea
- Mary Magdalene
- Thomas

John's Gospel differs in many ways from the Synoptic Gospels (Matthew, Mark, and Luke). John says nothing about Jesus' birth or temptation in the wilderness. It includes no parables and doesn't describe the Last Supper. On the other hand, well known stories such as the wedding at Cana and the raising of Lazarus are found only in John. But when we get to Jesus' trial and crucifixion, John has much in common with the other Gospels. Again, we see Jesus on trial before Pilate; and again Pilate gives the people the choice of releasing Jesus or Barabbas. Again Peter denies Jesus and again Jesus is buried by Joseph of Arimathea.

As you read, pay attention to how John's account of the trial and crucifixion is similar to and different from the accounts in the other Gospels.

- Based on your reading so far, how has John been different from the other Gospels?

- What details about Jesus' trial and crucifixion do you remember from the other Gospels?

2 NOW READ
JOHN 18–20.

3 Switchback

People look down on Thomas a lot. He had a hard time believing that someone who was dead magically appeared in a locked room and was now very much alive. As a result, he will forever be known as "Doubting Thomas." Can you really blame him for doubting? Would you have believed if you had been in his situation?

The first time we met Thomas in John's Gospel, he was hardly a doubter. In Chapter 11, after Jesus tells his disciples that they must go with him to Lazarus' home in Bethany, Thomas boldly declares, "Let us also go, that we may die with him" (11:16).

The Bible doesn't tell us what happens to Thomas after his experience with the risen Christ. Legend has it that Thomas traveled to India and started a church there, but historians cannot confirm this story. Several early Christian writings not included in the New Testament are attributed to Thomas (including the Gospel of Thomas), but scholars see little evidence that these works were actually written by Thomas. We may never know what happened to this disciple after he touched Jesus' wounds and believed.

• What evidence do you have that Jesus has died for our sins and risen from the dead? How much evidence do you need?

• When do you have doubts about your faith? How do you deal with those uncertainties?

4 Prayer

Jesus, we give you thanks for your sacrifice and for the good news of your resurrection. Be patient with us when we doubt, and give us the courage to tell the good news to others. Amen.

Feed My Sheep
John 21

1 Scouting the Terrain

Before wrapping up his time on earth, Jesus has a few more lessons in store for his disciples. In John 21, after a tumultuous week, Peter decides to go fishing. Fishing, after all, is what he knows best. Six of the other disciples join him. After a night at sea, the seven men had caught nothing.

Then Jesus shows up and things change. He tells the disciples to cast their net one more time; when they do, they catch so many fish that they cannot haul in the net. Peter is so excited by Jesus' appearance that he throws on some clothes, jumps in the water, and swims to the shore.

After breakfast on the beach, Jesus asks Peter three times—the same number of times that Peter denied Jesus—"Do you love me?" Jesus needs a threefold commitment from Peter because he knows the challenges that are in store for this disciple.

Trailblazers

- Jesus
- Peter
- the disciple whom Jesus loved
- the other disciples

• What activities do you enjoy doing when you are upset or overwhelmed? How do you feel God's presence when you do these activities?

WEEK
9
◈
DAY
5

2 NOW READ JOHN 21.

3 Switchback

Jesus asks Peter three times, "Do you love me?" Each time, Peter responds in the affirmative. And each time Jesus responds to Peter by saying, "Feed my lambs," "Tend my sheep," and "Feed my sheep," respectively. We know from John 10 that, when Jesus speaks of "lambs" and "sheep," he is speaking of us, God's children. So Jesus is essentially telling Peter, "If you truly love me, go out and serve and nurture others." We learned in Matthew 25:34-40 that whatever we do for others, we do for Jesus.

• How is loving others connected to loving Christ?

• In what ways can you "feed" or "tend" God's sheep?

Road Signs

• **Sea of Tiberius:** This was another name for the Sea of Galilee.
• **"A hundred fifty-three of them"** (21:11): The number 153 is the sum of the numbers 1 through 17 and may be symbolic of the expansion of the church.

John

Water Break

Congratulations, you've finished the Gospels and have read four takes on the life, death, and resurrection of Christ. Christ instructs his followers to "Go therefore and make disciples of all nations" (Matthew 28:19). Next week, we'll learn how Jesus' first followers responded to Jesus' instruction.

4 Prayer

God, you have given us the ability to do great things in your name. Guide us as we go forth to feed your sheep. Amen.

Part 2
Acts 1–2

1 Scouting the Terrain

Trailblazers

- Jesus
- Peter
- Matthias
- the other disciples
- the first converts

"The Acts of the Apostles" is the sequel to the Gospel of Luke. The same writer who told the story of Jesus' life is now telling the story of the life of the early church. While the Book of Luke begins with the birth of Jesus at Christmas, Acts begins with the birth of the church at Pentecost.

As you read Acts, you will notice that the leaders of the early church were far from perfect and that the ancient church—much like the church today—suffered from disputes about morality.

The story of the church begins in Jerusalem, the center of Judaism and the site of Jesus' death and resurrection. From Jerusalem, Acts follows church leaders to Syria, Cyprus, Asia, Macedonia, and throughout the known world. The book ends in Rome, the center of the Gentile world. Acts shows us how Christianity went from being a small, Jewish sect to being a worldwide faith.

- Acts tells the story of how the apostles continued the work that Jesus began. How does your congregation or youth ministry continue that work today?

NOW READ ACTS 1–2.

3 Switchback

As he did with the Gospel of Luke, Luke addresses Acts to "Theophilus." Theophilus is probably not an actual person. The Greek word *theo* means "God," and *philus* is similar to the Greek word for "lover." Thus Luke is writing his books for "God lovers."

Acts 2 tells the story of the first Christian Pentecost. Pentecost originated as a Jewish agricultural festival, also known as the Feast of Weeks, which fell on the fiftieth day after Passover. For Christians, Pentecost has become the day on which we celebrate the birth of the church and the outpouring of the Holy Spirit.

Acts 2:3 says that, on the day of Pentecost, "divided tongues, as of fire" rest on the disciples and that they are "filled with the Holy Spirit." In the nearly two millennia since these flames fell on the disciples, fire has become an important symbol of the Holy Spirit. Many congregations light candles during worship and dress their sanctuaries in red (a fiery color) during Pentecost.

• In what ways does your congregation recognize and celebrate Pentecost?

• How does your congregation use fire as a symbol?

Road Sign

• **"devout Jews from every nation"** (2:5): This phrase suggests that people outside of Galilee and Judea are hearing the gospel message. But they are still Jewish; the mission to the Gentiles has not yet begun.

4 Prayer

Gracious God, thank you for filling us with the Holy Spirit. Help us set the world on fire for you. Amen.

With Boldness
Acts 3–4

1 Scouting the Terrain

Peter hits the ground running as a leader of the newborn church. He has already preached a "fiery" sermon that resulted in 3,000 people being baptized and joining the church. Now, he's continuing Jesus' ministry of healing.

Peter and John meet a lame beggar at the gate of the Temple, and Peter heals the man in "the name of Jesus Christ of Nazareth." Although Jesus' power to heal has passed on to Peter, Peter has also inherited his teacher's ability to create controversy. Peter's miracle attracts so much attention that he and John must defend themselves to a council of priests and Sadducees. The council feels threatened by the disciples' boldness but can find no way to punish them and lets them go.

Trailblazers
- Peter
- John
- a beggar
- Barnabas
- Sadducees
- priests
- believers

- In what ways does the church today (and specifically your congregation or youth group) continue Jesus' ministry of healing?

2 NOW READ ACTS 3–4.

3 Switchback

The Temple authorities naively tell Peter and John to stop speaking, teaching, and healing in Jesus' name. These leaders likely fear that people will put their trust in Jesus' message of love, grace, and redemption and that they will turn away from the political and religious establishment.

We read over and again in the Gospels about the disciples' shortcomings. They miss the point of Jesus' teaching; they fall asleep when Jesus asks them to keep watch in the garden; Peter denies Jesus three times. In Acts, the disciples have changed: They now understand exactly who Jesus is and what he has called them to do, and they follow him boldly. In fact, they are recognized for their boldness (4:13), and they pray for boldness (4:23-31).

Dictionary.com defines *bold* as "not hesitating or fearful in the face of actual or possible danger or rebuff." Throughout history Christians have been bold in the face of danger or rebuff. Still today, many Christians boldly fight to end hunger and poverty, to improve people's lives, and to proclaim Christ's message.

• Whom do you know who follows Jesus with boldness? How?

• How can you boldly follow Christ?

Road Signs

• **"the captain of the temple"** (4:1): This officer kept order in the Temple and surrounding area. He was second in authority only to the high priest.
• **"John, and Alexander"** (4:6): Outside of Acts there are no records of these Temple leaders.

4 Prayer

Sovereign Lord, help us "speak your word with all boldness, while you stretch out your hand to heal, and signs and wonders are performed through the name of your holy servant Jesus" (Acts 4:29b-30).

Radical Obedience
Acts 5

1 Scouting the Terrain

The story of Ananias and Sapphira is a disturbing illustration of the importance of total fidelity to God. Toward the end of Chapter 4, we learn that the believers "were of one heart and soul, and no one claimed private ownership of any possessions, but everything they owned was held in common" (4:32). Ananias and Sapphira are two members of the early church who know that they should hand over everything they own to the apostles so that the apostles can distribute it accordingly. (See 4:35.)

Ananias, with the consent of Sapphira, his wife, sells some property and keeps part of the proceeds, instead of giving it all to the church. When Peter calls him out, Ananias drops dead. Hours later, Peter questions Sapphira, and she lies about the money her husband had withheld. As a result, she also dies.

The moral of this story is not "Give all your money to the church or you'll drop dead." Rather, the lesson is about being faithful to the commitments we make, particularly those we make in God's name.

• What commitments have you made to God? How faithful have you been to these commitments?

Trailblazers

• Peter
• the other apostles
• Ananias
• Sapphira
• Gamaliel
• high priest
• Sadducees

2 NOW READ ACTS 5.

3 Switchback

The apostles, it seems, avoid greater punishment thanks to the wisdom of a teacher of the Law, named Gamaliel. Gamaliel suggests that it's in the religious leaders' best interests to leave the apostles alone. He reasons that, if the apostles really are dangerous and deceptive, they will eventually fail; but, if the apostles are legitimate, the Temple authorities don't want to be "found fighting against God" (verse 39).

Throughout history, people who have been dismissed or condemned as troublemakers have made important contributions to the church. Such people have fought to abolish slavery, make education available to all, and eliminate corruption in the church and are responsible for founding many of the Christian denominations that are making a difference in the world today.

• When have prejudices kept you from listening to someone who had a good idea?

• Who are some historical "troublemakers" who ended up changing the world in important ways?

Road Signs

• **Theudas** (5:36-37): The Romans executed this self-proclaimed prophet when he gathered his large following at the Jordan River and told them that he could part the waters.
• **Judas the Galilean** (5:37): This insurrectionist led a revolt against Quirinius, governor of Syria, in A.D. 6.

4 Prayer

God, we give you thanks for the commitment of the apostles. We ask that you would help us achieve the same level of dedication to your word and work. Amen.

Fightin' Words
Acts 6–7

1 Scouting the Terrain

You may have noticed that a small number of apostles are doing a whole lot of work. And as the church continues to grow, the apostles' work is getting more difficult. As a result, the needs of the widows in the community are not being met. So the apostles, who need to devote themselves to "prayer and to serving the word" (6:4), select seven men to serve the members of the church.

The apostles recognize that the work of the church requires leadership from a lot of people with a variety of gifts. Someone who is skilled at preaching or evangelism is not necessarily good at tending to the needs of the sick or managing the church's food and money supply.

Healthy congregations today also rely on leadership and contributions from several people with diverse gifts, some of whom are clergy and paid staff and some of whom are lay volunteers.

Trailblazers
- the apostles
- Stephen
- six others chosen to serve
- members of the synagogue
- the council
- Saul

• Who are some of the leaders in your congregation or youth ministry? What different gifts do these people bring to the table?

• What gifts do you contribute to the church?

2 NOW READ ACTS 6–7.

WEEK
10

DAY
4

3 Switchback

The leaders of the early church have repeatedly clashed with the powers that be in Jerusalem, but so far none of them has been imprisoned or executed. However, that changes when Stephen, one of the seven chosen to serve in 6:1-7, is arrested for blasphemy.

We don't know exactly what Stephen does to get himself in trouble with the groups from the synagogue, only that these people falsely accuse him of threatening the Temple and the Law of Moses. Stephen responds to these charges with an impassioned speech in which he accuses the Temple leaders of being "stiff-necked" hypocrites who try to confine God to a place of worship.

This speech enrages Stephen's adversaries, and they respond by stoning him, making Stephen the first Christian martyr.

• How easy or difficult is being a Christian in today's world? How do the challenges that Christians today face compare with those the early church had to deal with?

• What do you know about places in the world where Christians are persecuted? How might being persecuted affect the way people follow Jesus?

4 Prayer

God of life and death, we give you thanks for the comfort you gave Stephen as he served you to the point of death. Show us ways that we can use our gifts to serve you, regardless of the cost. Amen.

Road Sign

• **"synagogue of the Freedmen" (6:9):** This group included Jewish former slaves from North Africa and Asia Minor.

Outcast Ministry
Acts 8

① Scouting the Terrain

In response to the persecution of the church in Jerusalem, Philip travels to Samaria. As you may recall from the Gospels, Jews and Samaritans had common ancestors but, because of disagreements over the Law and worship, didn't get along. Although Philip is Jewish, his message of grace and salvation and his ministry of healing resonate with the people of Samaria.

Trailblazers

- Philip
- Simon
- Peter
- John
- The Ethiopian

In Samaria we meet a character named Simon, a magician who has a large following among the Samaritans. When Simon sees the power of the Holy Spirit at work, he is amazed and asks the disciples if he can buy the Spirit's power. Although Simon repents, he appears as a bad guy in later Christian writings.

- In addition to the power of the Holy Spirit, what are some other great things that cannot be bought?

- How do we obtain these things?

②

**NOW READ
ACTS 8.**

③ Switchback

Acts includes several stories in which a powerful sermon or miraculous healing inspires an entire crowd of people to join the church. But the story of Philip and the Ethiopian reminds us that God also calls us to talk to people one-on-one about the good news of Christ. God actually instructs Philip to go out of his way to help one man better understand a passage from Isaiah. The man happens to be a servant of an Ethiopian queen, and he's studying Isaiah 53:7-8, in which the prophet describes the "suffering servant." Philip explains that this Scripture foreshadows the saving death of Jesus, and the Ethiopian asks to be baptized. The Ethiopian's conversion begins the church's mission to the Gentiles (non-Jewish, non-Samaritan people).

• What have you learned about God from a small-group Bible study or a conversation with another Christian?

④ Prayer

God of all people, open our eyes to new ways of communicating your message to all of your children. Amen.

Acts

Road Signs

• **Ethiopian:** In antiquity this term referred to anyone from the Upper Nile region south of Egypt.
• **The Candace:** This was a title for the queen of Meroe, a realm in current-day Sudan.

 In Matthew 20:19 Jesus tells the apostles to "Go therefore and make disciples of all nations." So far, they're off to a fast start. And they're using a lot of different techniques. Make a list of all of the ways so far that the apostles have let people know the good news of Christ. Then take a quiz at *www.amazingbiblerace.com* to show what you've learned.

Water Break

You've finished the first act of Acts. Take a breather and get ready to meet one of the most important figures in Christian history.

Starting Blocks
of the Church
Acts 9

① Scouting the Terrain

In chapters 7 and 8, we met a young man named Saul. We didn't learn much about him, except that he is notorious for persecuting the church.

Trailblazers

- Saul
- Ananias
- Barnabas
- Peter
- Tabitha
- the Hellenists

Now we meet Saul again, and he is "still breathing threats and murder against the disciples of the Lord" (9:1). He plans a trip to Damascus in Syria, with the intent of delivering letters to the synagogues there, warning them not to become a safe haven for Christians. But on his way to Damascus, Saul has an encounter with Jesus and everything changes. A light from heaven renders Saul blind and enables him to see the error of his ways.

From this point on, Saul, who had been one of the church's most strident adversaries, becomes one of the church's most important leaders.

• When have you had an "eye-opening" experience that changed your behavior or your attitude toward something? What happened?

• What other biblical persons have you read about who had an experience similar to Saul's?

② NOW READ ACTS 9.

3 Switchback

Saul doesn't hesitate to embrace his new role as an evangelist for Christ. Although his bold preaching in Damascus and Jerusalem is effective, it is also controversial. When Saul's adversaries threaten his life, others in church send him to his hometown of Tarsus.

The change of scenery is good for Saul and for the rest of the church. When Saul leaves, the controversy that had surrounded him dies down; and the apostles are able to continue building up the church. Meanwhile, Saul is in Tarsus, a center of culture and commerce on the northeastern curve of the Mediterranean Sea and the perfect place for Saul to prepare for his mission to Gentiles throughout the Roman world.

• When have you had to walk away from a difficult or dangerous situation? What happened to you and to the people you left behind when you did?

Road Signs

• **The Way** (9:2): Before the name "Christian" came into being, "The Way" was a common name for the church.
• **Hellenists** (9:29): These were Greek-speaking Jews.

Acts

 When the disciple Tabitha falls ill and dies, Peter restores her to life. (Tabitha's Greek name is Dorcas.) So far in Acts, the apostles have performed several great miracles. Look back over the first 9 chapters and find as many miracles as you can. How many did you come up with? Test what you've learned by taking a quiz at *www.amazingbiblerace.com*.

4 Prayer

God of redemption, help us turn our lives around when we're headed in the wrong direction. Show us where we need to go and whom we need to serve in your name. Amen.

Revolutionary Dream
Acts 10–11

1 Scouting the Terrain

Acts 10 reminds us that, even though the New Testament sometimes tells us that "the Jews" are the apostles' adversaries, the disciples are themselves faithful Jews who obey the Jewish Law. So Peter is understandably confused when he has a dream in which God commands him to eat animals that Jewish Law considers unclean. (You may remember the rules against eating these animals from Leviticus 11:24-47.) When Peter objects to eating "profane" and "unclean" animals, God replies, "What God has made clean, you must not call profane" (10:15).

Although Peter's dream will later have an impact on the church's debate over food laws, it is really more about people than about food. Peter has reservations about meeting with Cornelius, a Roman centurion and a Gentile who doesn't observe Jewish Law. But, explains Peter, "God has shown me that I should not call anyone profane or unclean" (10:28).

Trailblazers

- **Peter**
- **Cornelius**
- **Barnabas**
- **Saul**
- **Agabus**
- **Gentiles**

- Peter is reluctant to tell Cornelius about Jesus because Cornelius is a Gentile. For what reasons are you reluctant to talk to someone about your faith?

2 NOW READ ACTS 10–11.

3 Switchback

The earliest Christians were Jewish. They believed that Jesus had fulfilled the Jewish Scriptures and they continued to worship in the Temple and observe Jewish law. But now, following Peter's vision of the animals, the apostles have begun preaching to Gentile, several of whom are joining the church. Some of these Gentiles are familiar with Judaism and already worship the God of Israel; others are completely new to the faith.

Historians can point to no moment when Christianity "officially" split from Judaism. For several decades after Christ's resurrection, there were still people who referred to themselves as Jewish Christians or Christian Jews. But the mission to the Gentiles that begins in Acts is the event largely responsible for the eventual separation of Judaism and Christianity.

• What do you know about the similarities and differences between Judaism and Christianity?

• What questions do you have about the relationship between Judaism and Christianity? To whom could you go for answers?

Road Sign

• "the disciples were first called 'Christians'" (11:26): This is where the name "Christian," which essentially means "little Christ," makes its first appearance. The people of Antioch give the disciples this name, possibly to poke fun at them.

4 Prayer

God of the entire world, your church spans the globe. Thank you for the disciples who first had the courage to tell Gentiles about the good news of Christ. Help Christians of all ethnicities and nationalities come together to do the work of your kingdom. Amen.

Persecution in the Church
Acts 12–14

1 Scouting the Terrain

Now things are getting dangerous. King Herod has the apostle James killed (12:2) and Peter arrested. Stephen has already been stoned to death for preaching the Gospel, and the church's adversaries are doing everything they can to thwart the apostles' ministry. But this intense opposition doesn't slow down the apostles' efforts to tell people about Jesus. Their mission spreads to cities such as Antioch and Iconium (in current-day Turkey) and to Cyprus.

Saul—whom we learn is also known as Paul—and Barnabas have taken the lead in preaching to Jews and Gentiles outside Jerusalem, and the two of them have some interesting adventures. In Cyprus they render a magician named Elymas, who interferes with their work, temporarily blind; in Antioch of Pisidia their religious adversaries instigate a battle of the sexes and the two apostles leave the city in protest; in Lystra, Paul and Barnabas are mistaken for Greek gods (Zeus and Hermes, respectively), and Paul is nearly stoned to death. Despite all of the drama, many people in all of these cities join the church.

Trailblazers

- James
- Peter
- King Herod
- Rhoda
- Barnabas
- Saul
- Elymas
- a man crippled from birth

• When have negative criticism and opposition inspired you to work harder?

• What unusual or incredible adventures have you had? What impact have these experiences had on your faith?

2 NOW READ ACTS 12–14.

3 Switchback

Now that you've read nearly five-sixths of the Bible, miracles probably seem commonplace. By this time, you've seen a river turn to blood, a disembodied hand write a message on a wall, people healed of all sorts of illnesses, and a man raised to life after being dead for four days. Just as runners who jog by the same beautiful scenery every day eventually neglect to notice how spectacular it is, we sometimes do the same thing when reading about incredible events in the Bible.

The story of Peter's miraculous escape from jail may keep us from becoming too jaded when it comes to miracles. Peter's fellow Christians are well aware of how dire his situation is. Herod, who had just had the apostle James killed, has assigned "four squads of soldiers" to guard Peter, who is already bound in chains. When Peter shows up at Mary's house, after an angel had miraculously delivered him from maximum-security lockdown, Rhoda the servant girl is so flabbergasted that she forgets to open the door for Peter, leaving him outside while she runs to tell everyone in the household.

Rhoda's excitement is a reminder to us not to become so jaded that we lose our sense of awe and wonder.

• Which biblical miracles impress you most? Why?

• What amazing acts of God have you witnessed?

Road Signs

• **Bar-Jesus** (13:6): This name for Elymas means "son of Jesus." Jesus was a common Jewish name in the first century.
• **"They tore their clothes"** (14:14): Tearing one's clothes was a common response to blasphemy.

4 Prayer

God of surprise, grant us fresh eyes so that we can see your glory as if it were for the first time. Keep our passion from crusting over by our desire for something new. Amen.

Christian Conferencing
Acts 15–16

1 Scouting the Terrain

The account of the Council at Jerusalem in Acts 15 gives us an early example of a very important Christian practice: conferencing. Christian conferencing is the way that the church makes decisions as a community. Most churches today practice some sort of community-wide decision-making. Baptist churches meet in conventions, Lutherans meet in Synods, United Methodists meet in Annual and General Conferences. The Pope consults with the Council of Cardinals or will sometimes call church-wide councils like Vatican II or The Council of Trent.

Trailblazers

- Paul
- Barnabas
- Peter
- James
- Silas
- Timothy
- Lydia
- the jailer

Through conferencing, Christians utilize the gifts that God has given to us to make community-wide decisions. We bring to the table our knowledge of Scripture, our experience of how God has worked in our lives, and the witness of other Christians throughout history. God has blessed us all with reason so that we can process and apply all of this information. As you read Acts 15, look for ways in which the apostles meeting in Jerusalem use Scripture, experience, tradition, and reason to come to a decision.

WEEK
11
◆
DAY
4

• How do your congregation and youth group make decisions as a group? How do you use Scripture, experience, tradition, and reason?

fast forward Get permission to sit in on a council or committee meeting at your church. Take notes and discuss your experience as a team. Write about the meeting on your race blog or film a video reenactment of the meeting and upload it at *www.amazingbiblerace.com.*

2 NOW READ ACTS 15–16.

③ Switchback

Paul and his companions Timothy and Silas aren't working off of an itinerary. Instead, they go where the Holy Spirit leads them. Acts 16:6 tells us that the Spirit forbids the three men "to speak the word in Asia," so they avoid that region. As they are spending the night in the harbor city of Troas, Paul has a dream about a "man of Macedonia" who asks for help. "Immediately," Paul and company set sail across the Aegean Sea to Macedonia.

By following the Holy Spirit and responding to his vision of the man of Macedonia, Paul takes the Christian mission into Europe. With Lydia's help, he starts the first European church in Philippi.

• How do you know when the Holy Spirit wants you to do something (or not do something)?

• When have you dropped everything to help someone who needed you? What happened?

④ Prayer

Holy Spirit, guide our paths so that we might do the work you have set before us. Amen.

In Leg 4 you filled out a Minor Prophets scorecard. Now you're going to be scouting some new talent. Check out *www.amazingbiblerace.com* to find the Scouting Report for Paul's churches. Enter the information you've learned about the church in Philippi into the report and earn extra points.

Road Signs

• **Asia:** This refers not to the continent but to the Roman province of the same name. Asia was located in the western part of current-day Turkey

• **"a worshiper of God"** (16:14): This phrase refers to a Gentile who worshiped the God of Israel.

Acts

Scouting Report
Acts 17–18

① Scouting the Terrain

The names of the cities where Paul and his companions are starting churches may sound familiar. Yesterday, you read about the church in Philippi. Today you'll read about the churches in Thessalonica, Corinth, and Ephesus. These churches are recipients of Paul's famous letters (Philippians, 1 and 2 Thessalonians, and 1 and 2 Corinthians, respectively), letters that you'll read in Leg 6 of the Amazing Bible Race.

As you read about each of Paul's churches, pay attention to where the church is located, Paul's message to the church, any prominent figures in the church, and anything that makes the church unique. Make a note of whether each church is made up of Jews, Gentiles, or both. All of the studying you do now will pay off in Leg 6.

- If Paul were to write a letter or preach a sermon to your congregation or youth group, what might he say? What would he commend you for doing well? What would he say needs to change?

Trailblazers

- Paul
- Silas
- Timothy
- Jason
- Priscilla and Aquila
- Greeks
- Jews
- Apollos
- Gallio
- Sosthenes
- believers
- philosophers

WEEK
11
◆
DAY
5

hurdle Update your Scouting Report to include information about the churches in Thessalonica, Corinth, and Ephesus at *amazingbiblerace.com*.

② NOW READ ACTS 17–18.

3 Switchback

The Areopagus in Athens was where people went to argue, debate, discuss, preach, and learn. It was the town square of one of the most intellectual cities in all of history. Acts tells us that people of many religious and philosophical persuasions went there to discuss matters of God and truth.

Paul is able to reach out to his audience in Athens, because he has taken the time to learn about their culture. He spies an altar bearing the inscription, "To an unknown god" (17:23) and suggests that this unknown god is none other than the one true God—the God manifest in Christ.

Paul takes a serious look at Greek pagan culture and sees a glimpse of God. Many Christians today follow Paul's lead by looking for Christian themes in secular books, movies, sports, and music.

• When have you seen God at work in an unexpected place?

• What Christian themes and messages can you find in your favorite books, movies, sports, and music?

4 Prayer

God of all people, thank you for always being present with us. Help us to seek and find you everywhere we go. Amen.

Road Sign

• **Priscilla and Aquila** (18:18, 26): Placing a woman's name (Priscilla) before a man's (Aquila) was rare in antiquity. Priscilla was likely of higher social or economic standing than her companion.

Water Break

One week to go! Rest up, because Paul and company still have several adventures and challenges ahead.

Drama in Ephesus
Acts 19–20

1 Scouting the Terrain

At the beginning of Acts 19, Paul encounters people in Ephesus who have been baptized in the baptism of John but not of Jesus. Why isn't the baptism of John enough? Indeed, Jesus was baptized by John and did not baptize himself again following his baptism. Yet Paul insists that the Corinthians must be baptized in the baptism of Jesus. What's the difference?

John's baptism was a baptism of repentance. It was about asking God to forgive one's sins and promising to live in a more righteous way. While there is nothing wrong with such a baptism, Christian baptism goes one step further. It signifies that a person has been equipped by the Holy Spirit to be a part of God's new creation: a creation that began with Jesus' resurrection on Easter.

Trailblazers

- **Paul**
- **Timothy**
- **Paul's other companions**
- **disciples in Ephesus**
- **sons of Sceva**
- **Demetrius**
- **Ephesian elders**

• Have you been baptized? If so, what do you know or remember about your baptism? If not, what questions do you have about baptism?

2 NOW READ ACTS 19–20.

3 Switchback

The gospel was not just a threat to the religious establishment, it was also a threat to local economies. Demetrius, a silversmith in Ephesus, was well aware that pagan idol worship kept many tradespeople in business. By inviting people to follow Christ and leave their idols behind, Paul becomes a threat to the entire idol-making industry in Ephesus. The artisans get so upset that a riot nearly ensues, but the town clerk intervenes and reminds the people that Paul and his companions have broken no laws.

Acts 20 tells a story that should resonate with anyone who has ever dozed off during church. Eutychus, a young man in Troas, falls asleep listening to Paul's sermon and falls out of the window to his death. Paul quickly restores him to life, demonstrating that God has sympathy for people who drift off during long-winded sermons.

• How can you, like the town clerk, act as a peacemaker among your friends and peers?

• Have you ever fallen asleep during church? What can you or some other sleepyhead do to stay more alert during worship?

Road Sign

• **"Artemis of the Ephesians"** (19:28): The Greek goddess Artemis was very important to the Ephesians. The temple of Artemis in Ephesus was one of the Seven Wonders of the Ancient World.

4 Prayer

God, keep us awake to hear your word and act on it so that others might learn about you through us. Amen.

Paul the Celebrity
Acts 21–22

1 Scouting the Terrain

Paul travels from city to city, like a rock star on tour. Wherever he goes, people recognize him, flock to him, and offer to take care of him.

Of course, being a celebrity has a down side. In Jerusalem, James—Jesus' brother and the head of the church in Jerusalem—convinces Paul to go through the Jewish purification rites in the Temple. Paul has wrongly gotten a reputation for being anti-Jewish, and doing the purification rites will help his reputation among the many Jewish Christians in Jerusalem. But when Paul enters the Temple, many of his adversaries recognize the celebrity in their midst. They are angry about Paul's teaching on Judaism and his work among the Gentiles, so they have him arrested. Several trials and speeches follow.

- Have you ever dreamed of being a celebrity? What would be the benefits? What would be the drawbacks?

Trailblazers

- **Paul**
- **Philip**
- **Agabus**
- **Mnason (NAY-suhn)**
- **James**
- **the crowd in Jerusalem**
- **the tribune in Jerusalem**
- **the Roman tribune**

2 NOW READ ACTS 21–22.

3 Switchback

Paul's journey to Jerusalem was either exceptionally brave or exceptionally foolish. As he travels to Jerusalem, several people warn him not to go. A prophet named Agabus even binds his hands and feet with Paul's belt as a warning. But Paul goes anyway.

We cannot know whether Paul went to Jerusalem, expecting to be arrested or assuming that God would protect him from his adversaries. Whatever the case, Paul went into Jerusalem, with tremendous faith, and never wavered from his call to preach the good news of Christ.

- When have you done something even though several people told you not to? Why did you do it?

- Do you think that Paul was wise or foolish for going to Jerusalem? Why?

Road Signs

- **"He had four unmarried daughters who had the gift of prophecy"** (21:9): This detail about Philip's daughters adds nothing to the story but confirms the promise in 2:17-18 that both men and women, sons and daughters would prophesy.
- **The Egyptian** (21:38): This religious leader led a revolt against Rome sometime between A.D. 52 and 59.

4 Prayer

God, help us to follow you, to have the courage to pursue missions that others might think are foolish and the wisdom to avoid the roads that truly are foolish. Amen.

On Trial
Acts 23–24

① Scouting the Terrain

Hostilities are growing not only between the Temple and the Roman authorities but also within the Temple. The two sects that held most of the power in the Temple, the Pharisees and Sadducees, had fundamental disagreements about the resurrection of the body. (Pharisees believed in it; Sadducees didn't.) The Pharisees were popular among the people; the Sadducees were well-connected.

Paul, a former Pharisee, knows exactly what buttons to push and manages to get the Pharisees and Sadducees to fight with each other. When things start getting violent, the tribune steps in to protect Paul. This is one of many instances in chapters 23–24 where Paul narrowly escapes from a dangerous situation.

- What issues divide groups within the church today? Why are people so passionate about these issues?

WEEK
12
◇
DAY
3

Trailblazers

- Paul
- Felix
- Drusilla
- the Roman tribune
- Pharisees
- Sadducees
- the son of Paul's sister
- Ananias
- Tertullus

②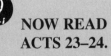
NOW READ ACTS 23–24.

3 Switchback

Paul's fiasco at the Temple, in Chapter 21, has gotten him an audience with some of the region's most powerful political and religious leaders. He has already told his story to the Jewish Temple authorities; now he appears before Felix, the Roman governor of Judea and makes his case once again.

At no point during these trials does Paul seem intimidated, and at no point does he waver from his hope in God or faith in Christ. Even though he is wrongly imprisoned—Felix seems to fear that Paul will stir up trouble—Paul keeps his composure.

• How, do you think, did Paul keep his composure when he was on trial?

• When, if ever, have you been tempted to waver from your faith? What did you do?

Acts

Road Signs

• **Claudius Lysias** (23:26): This is the name of the Roman tribune who has been unnamed up to this point.
• **Drusilla** (24:24): She was both Felix's wife and King Herod Agrippa I's daughter.

4 Prayer

Amazing God, help us keep our composure during the trials of life. Thank you for the example and witness of Paul, who never wavered in his faith. Amen.

 Find a map of the ancient Mediterranean world and map out Paul's travels in Acts 19–28. Mark each of the cities he visits and his route from one place to the next. Then go to *www.amazingbiblerace.com* and take a quiz about what you've learned.

123

Passed Around
Acts 25–26

1 Scouting the Terrain

Trailblazers
- Paul
- Festus
- Agrippa
- Bernice

After waiting in prison for two years, Paul is passed from one governor to the next. The new governor, Festus, like Felix before him, doesn't know what to do with Paul and sends him on to King Herod Agrippa II.

In a lengthy speech, Paul defends himself before the king: He tells the story of his conversion and of his life as an apostle. He even appeals to the king to believe in Christ.

After Paul has finished making his appeal, Agrippa decides that the apostle has done "nothing to deserve death or imprisonment" (26:31). Agrippa is prepared to release Paul, but Paul has already requested to defend himself before the Emperor of Rome.

• When, if ever, have you had to defend yourself against false accusations? Did you want to speak to the person in charge? Why, or why not?

WEEK
12
◆
DAY
4

2 NOW READ ACTS 25–26

③ Switchback

You may have noticed that we haven't heard from Peter or the other original disciples for quite a while. We briefly caught up with Philip and James in Chapter 21, but much of the second half of Acts has focused on Paul. Even when the focus of the story returns to Jerusalem and Paul spends two entire years in jail, Luke doesn't tell us anything about what the disciples in Jerusalem have been doing.

Acts begins by telling the story of the church in Jerusalem and ends by telling the story of Paul. This shift in Luke's story reflects a broader shift in the church. At first, the church was largely a Jewish movement in Jerusalem; but within a few decades, the church had become a largely Gentile movement that spanned the Roman Empire.

• What have you found most interesting or inspiring about Paul's story?

• In what ways does your congregation reach out to new groups of people?

fast forward

Paul spends a lot of time on trial in the final chapters of Acts.

As a team, take a trip to a nearby courthouse when court is in session. Pay special attention to the key players in the trial and what is at stake. For points, on your race blog, compare this courtroom experience to Paul's trials in Acts.

Or select one of Paul's trials and reenact it in a contemporary setting, with a prosecutor, a defense attorney, witnesses, and a jury. Produce a video of your trial and upload it at *www.amazingbiblerace.com* for points.

④ Prayer

God, help us follow the example of Paul who was able to bridge boundaries of language and culture to spread the gospel. Amen.

Avast, Ye Land Lubbers!
Acts 27–28

1 Scouting the Terrain

Luke's story of Paul's voyage from Jerusalem to Rome is impressive in its detail. You may notice that parts of today's reading (like some previous passages in Acts) are told in the first person (using "we" instead of "they"). This has led some to believe that the author was on the boat with Paul.

Trailblazers

- Paul
- soldiers and sailors
- Publius
- Jewish leaders in Rome

Paul's sea voyage turns out to be just as tumultuous as his travels on land. The boat is pounded by storms and blown off course: Paul and the soldiers and crew accompanying him are lost at sea, hoping to "run aground on some island" (27:25). After about two weeks, as the sailors suspect that the boat is nearing land, some of the soldiers try to escape on the life boat, leaving everyone else to fend for themselves. But Paul, who has made an impression on their commanding officer thwarts their plan.

Finally, the boat wrecks on the shore of Malta, an island south of Sicily in the Mediterranean Sea, where Paul's mission continues.

- What "storms" have you faced? Where did you find strength and courage during these times?

2 NOW READ ACTS 27–28.

③ Switchback

The ending of Acts may seem anticlimactic. After a dangerous voyage, years of preparation, and tremendous difficulty, Paul finally makes it to Rome. But we never get to see Paul make his appeal before the emperor.

Still, the fact that Acts concludes with Paul preaching in Rome is significant. Luke's first book began with Jesus' birth in a stable outside of Bethlehem. His second book ends with one of the church's greatest leaders preaching Jesus' message in the capital of the known world. Christianity has come a long way in a short time.

• What is the most fascinating thing you've learned about the early church from reading Acts?

• How does the church today continue the apostles' mission?

④ Prayer

Help us, great God, continue the ministry of Paul, Priscilla, Luke, Barnabus, Timothy, Dorcas, Mary, the disciples, and most of all—Jesus Christ. Amen.

Road Signs

• **"because even the Fast had already gone by"** (27:9): The "Fast" is the Day of Atonement, which falls in September or October. Sea voyages after this time of year were often dangerous because of bad weather.
• **sea anchor** (27:17): This is a very sturdy sail that is lowered into the water to slow a ship.
• **fifteen fathoms** (27:28): This depth is equal to about 90 feet.

Water Break

Five legs done and only one to go! You've read almost the entire Bible! Get some rest, then grab your letter opener because you'll be reading a lot of letters in Leg 6.

AMAZING BIBLE RACE
Team Covenant

As a member of _____
(Team Name)

in The Amazing Bible Race, I make this covenant to read my daily

Bible readings, read my Runner's Reader, and answer the reflection

questions. I commit to supporting my teammates and being held

accountable by them for doing all I can do to make the most of this

experience. I will be present at team meetings and youth group.

I am determined to grow in my knowledge of God's Word in my

personal faith journey.

_____   _____
(Signature)   (Date)

Have team members sign below and put their contact information
(e-mail address, phone numbers, text addresses, and IM names) nearby.